Praise for *Getting Ahead*

"So many executives I know are always looking for ways to take their careers to the next level. Joel Garfinkle shows them how in *Getting Ahead*. By focusing on three key aspects—perception, visibility, and influence—this book presents a compelling case for what an executive needs to do to become a more credible leader. Each chapter ends with handy summary steps that readers can put into gear for themselves. *Getting Ahead* is a welcome read for anyone seeking to advance his or her career."

—**John Baldoni**
Author of *Lead Your Boss:*
The Subtle Art of Managing Up

"*Getting Ahead* delivers. Definitely providing a step-up and step-ahead perspective on how to make a difference and get recognized for doing so, it is full of practical ideas and applications for managing a career without the customary politics and b.s.! This book is an enjoyable and fresh read with a lot of interesting examples."

—**Barry Z. Posner, PhD**
Professor of leadership at Santa Clara University
Coauthor of *The Leadership Challenge*, *Credibility*,
and *The Truth about Leadership*

"The book is chock-full of quotes, cases, ideas, and tools. Anyone who wants to get ahead will find this book thorough, well written, easy to read, and quickly applicable."

—**Dave Ulrich**
Coauthor of *The Why of Work*
Professor, Ross School of Business,
University of Michigan

"Joel Garfinkle offers smart strategies to stand out from the crowd—which is extremely important if you want to build an influential network and move forward quickly in your career. He wraps the strategy in riveting stories and offers practical advice. I like this book."

—**Keith Ferrazzi**
Author of *Who's Got Your Back* and *Never Eat Alone*

"This book provides tremendous insight into who you are and how you can have a bigger impact on those around you. If you're really serious about boosting your career, reading *Getting Ahead* will be one of the best moves you can make."

—**Sydney Finkelstein**
Professor, Tuck School of Business, Dartmouth College
Author of the best seller *Why Smart Executives Fail*

"*Getting Ahead* is a book that will help you manage your career. Joel Garfinkle provides practical, actionable ideas you can use to get ahead. The book delivers on its promise."

—**Mark Sanborn**
Author of *The Fred Factor* and
You Don't Need a Title to Be a Leader

"Good ambition is a great asset. This book helps you put that ambition to work."

—**Jim Champy**
Coauthor of *Reengineering the Corporation*

"*Getting Ahead* breaks down success into three profoundly simple principles to systematically and pragmatically elevate your career. Joel Garfinkle gives you the tools to be an exceptional difference maker and value creator in our complex, dynamic world."

—**Kevin Cashman**
Best-selling author of *Leadership from the Inside Out*
and *Awakening the Leader Within*

"In this insightful book, Joel Garfinkle provides his brilliant PVI model to help you gain the competitive advantage needed in today's marketplace."

—**Jon Gordon**
Best-selling author of *The Energy Bus* and *Soup*

"*Getting Ahead* is a must-have resource to accelerate and advance as a global leader. The powerful three-step process clearly outlines what a leader must do to maximize his or her potential. It provides practical advice for leadership development and is a must read."

—**Phil Harkins**
CEO, Linkage, Inc.

"*Getting Ahead* lays out, in very straightforward terms, a simple and practical model that leaders can use to seize the reins of their own careers while identifying and supporting the essential development of their employees."

—**Beverly Kaye**
Coauthor of *Love 'Em or Lose 'Em*

Getting
AHEAD

Getting AHEAD

THREE STEPS
to TAKE YOUR CAREER to
the NEXT LEVEL

Joel A. Garfinkle

WILEY

John Wiley & Sons, Inc.

For general information on our other products and services or for technical support, please contact our Customer Care Department within the United States at (800) 762-2974, outside the United States at (317) 572-3993 or fax (317) 572-4002.

Wiley also publishes its books in a variety of electronic formats. Some content that appears in print may not be available in electronic books. For more information about Wiley products, visit our web site at www.wiley.com.

ISBN: 978-0-470-91587-5 (cloth)
ISBN: 978-1-118-11675-3 (ebk)
ISBN: 978-1-118-11676-0 (ebk)
ISBN: 978-1-118-11677-7 (ebk)

Printed in the United States of America

10 9 8 7 6 5 4 3 2 1

To my beloved wife Jueli,

*"From every human being there rises
a light that reaches straight to heaven.
And when two souls that are destined to
be together find each other, their streams
of light flow together and a single, brighter
light goes forth from their united being."*

The Baal Shem Tov

Contents

Foreword

In *Getting Ahead: Three Steps to Take Your Career to the Next Level,* Joel Garfinkle hits upon three significant and important aspects of leadership—perception, visibility, and influence. Like Joel, I stress developing perception or taking control of how others see you (your reputation) and exerting your influence no matter what level you are at in the organization (effectively influencing up) as an integral part of my own leadership philosophy.

With this book, Joel takes us on an incredible learning journey in his exploration of taking control of how others see us—or our reputation. Our reputation, what other people think we've done lately, is basically a scorecard kept about us by others. It's when our coworkers, customers, friends, and sometimes strangers grade our performance—and report their opinions to the rest of the world. Although you can't take total control of your reputation, there's a lot you can do to maintain and improve it. Joel explores this concept to its fullest here in *Getting Ahead.*

Another fascinating aspect of leadership explored in *Getting Ahead* is exerting influence in the organization—no matter what level you are at! Peter Drucker once said, "The great majority of people tend to focus downward. They are occupied with efforts rather than results. They worry over what the organization and their superiors 'owe' them and should do for them. And they are conscious above all of the authority they 'should have.' As a result they render themselves ineffectual." The fact of the matter is, though, that every decision is made by the person who has the power to make that decision—this is not necessarily the right person or the smartest person or the best person—and this is something with which we all must make peace. Making peace with this fact will inevitably help you do a much better job of influencing decision makers, which will, along with all of the teachings you'll learn in this book, help you to convert your good ideas into meaningful action.

As Joel says, "performing to the best of your ability is necessary at every level of your career." And this is a book that will help you do just that. Whether you are a new employee, in middle or upper management, a CEO, or a future leader, take in the information Joel has put in these pages, apply his PVI (perception, visibility, influence) model to your own career and organization, and watch as changes happen and you experience the heights of career success!

—**Marshall Goldsmith**
Executive coach and best-selling author of *Mojo*
and *What Got You Here Won't Get You There*

Acknowledgments

This book is a dream come true. I am thrilled to bring this book into the world. To create a book that I would love to read is the ultimate joy. My gratitude is to the quality of people who contributed to turning this book into something outstanding.

Most important, to my wife, whom I love deeply. I am so blessed to have you as a partner. Your growth as a human being and unwavering dedication to the depths of who you truly are inspire me. I love your beauty, depth, wisdom, care, and touch. Your spark for life is infectious. Our children know what love is because of you. Our partnership is full of fun, truth, laughter, play, honesty, love, spirit, realness, and connection. I love you.

No one has contributed more to my life and this book than my wife. She helped plan, organize, and develop the book. She was dedicated to making sure the flow, structure, and cohesiveness were attended to. Besides being my book doctor, she was a constant sounding board throughout the process. Jueli, thank you for your unwavering ocean of support and expertise. I am blessed to have such a generous, brilliant, and loving partner.

My deep appreciation and respect go to a select group of dear friends and coaching clients who, as manuscript readers, provided exceptional insights and wisdom. Each of you brilliantly defines leadership in your professional lives. Thank you for making the time in your busy and demanding schedules to help me achieve my goals with this project: Eric Antebi, Marni Taradash, Butler Rondeno, Kara Gilbert, Stuart Glaun, Hannah

Hieu, and Rekha Rao Mayya. I am indebted to you for your generous amount of time and attention.

Heartfelt thanks to: Michele Lisenbury Christensen for her creative ideas and support; Jack Sommars, whose edits always prove invaluable; Darren Verbout, who provided the excellent graphics; and Dick Bolles for his love, support, and friendship.

Thank you to Lauren Murphy at John Wiley & Sons, Inc., for being the person who found me. This book wouldn't have happened if you didn't do your job well. As my editor, I have appreciated your ideas, perspective, and guidance. Thanks also to the other hardworking, committed, and supportive people at Wiley, especially Christine Moore and Susan Moran.

Harold Goldstein, my cousin, friend, and holy-brother on this planet: Thank you for being the first person to see me, believe in me, and love me deeply. For my entire life I have felt an unwavering and constant heartfelt connection. Our conversations for the past 25 years are some of the most supportive aspects of my life.

K'vod Wieder, my friend and holy-brother: Our friendship has grown into something truly special. Our weekly conversations are grounding, loving, and deeply transformative. The honesty that we share brings a depth to knowing our inner selves at the ultimate level. Thank you.

Deep appreciation to my parents, Jack and Arlene, for providing constant encouragement and support. You have always been a solid presence in my life.

Ariella Joy and Haydn Kol, my two children: You bring a tremendous amount of purpose and aliveness to all that you do. I am lifted up by your presence. I feel blessed to have such beautiful, curious, intelligent, and joyful children. You inspire me to be a doting and present father.

Introduction

We cannot become what we need to be by remaining what we are.

—Max De Pree
Writer, industrialist, former CEO of Herman Miller, Inc.

What Makes One Person More Successful than Another?

Who comes to mind when you hear the phrase *successful leaders*? Do you think of someone you work with now? Are these leaders people from your past employment? Or are they individuals you've only seen from afar or read about? Do you know how

> *The most successful leaders have gotten to where they are by leveraging and applying perception, visibility, and influence better than anyone else.*

these successful leaders advanced and achieved the promotions they desired, or how they became recognized as being highly capable, credible, and respected by upper management? Perhaps the most pressing question is: ***What do they do that is so different than what you are doing?*** You search for the answers, wondering what the secret ingredient is and how you can get your hands on it. You want to know what makes one person more successful than another, or—more bluntly—exactly what these people have that you don't.

The answer: perception, visibility, and influence.

The most successful leaders have gotten to where they are by leveraging and applying perception, visibility, and influence better than anyone else. By honing these three areas, you too can fast-track to the next level and become both a valued employee and an in-demand leader.

You've likely heard throughout your career that you perform your job well, produce exceptional results, are smart, are extremely competent, and have a desired expertise. You might be surprised, however, that this kind of recognition hasn't necessarily guaranteed your success. The reality you face at work is that talent, results, and competence alone simply will not allow you to attain the success you deserve. It's time to stop being surprised by this, and instead take control of your professional future.

If you want to take your career up a notch, this book will provide you with a model to do exactly that. The best part is that you'll start from where you are right now—by tackling all of the professional struggles, issues, challenges, and deep-seated habits that have been so hard to overcome. This book provides a step-by-step program that will push you to surpass whatever is in your way and remove your limiting career blind spots.

> *The reality you face at work is that talent, results, and competence alone simply will not allow you to attain the success you deserve.*

No matter what you've achieved at work over the years, your current position is your starting point. You now need the:

- *Commitment* to change.
- *Willingness* to do whatever is required.
- *Dedication* to reach your desired level.
- *Courage* to stay steadfast.
- *Ability* to take the necessary steps forward even in the face of fear.

By tapping into these elements of strength within you, you form a powerful energy source that will propel you to career heights you never before deemed possible. Yes, it will be difficult. You'll be inspired and energized, however, by the immediate results you achieve as you begin to apply the PVI model—perception, visibility, and influence—to your work.

You *can* do this. I know because I see it happen all the time. The experiences of hundreds of my clients have proven how quickly positive changes in work situations can occur. They conquered challenges that initially seemed impossible to overcome, and arrived at levels they were not expected to reach. They did so by working according to a vital realization: that improving how others perceive you, increasing your visibility, and exerting influence are the exact factors that determine your future success.

This book has three parts that we are about to look at in more detail:

- Part One: Improve Your Perception
- Part Two: Increase Your Visibility
- Part Three: Exert Your Influence

Based on your current career circumstances, you might find yourself drawn to one part more than another. By itself each part provides value. However, formed together—as the PVI model—is how this book is meant to be understood. Transformation and advancement of your career come from the complete implementation of the PVI model (see Figure I.1).

Improve Your Perception
Create the right image of yourself by taking control of how others see you, so that the perception of you accurately reflects your impact on the organization.

People constantly are forming opinions of you based on how you act, what you do, and how you behave at work. These

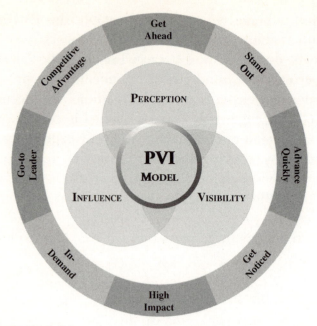

FIGURE I.1 PVI Model

impressions have a direct impact on how you are perceived. Others' positive or negative discernment of you affects myriad elements of interaction—how they treat you, the level of respect you receive, and the overall success you gain at work. This is precisely why perception management is vital to your professional success. If you don't take control of how others see you, you will undermine both your career and your future success. People will form opinions about you without any input from you. You can't leave the fate of your career in someone else's hands.

Increase Your Visibility

Increase your profile across the organization and among higher levels of management by standing out and getting noticed.

Visibility makes you a known, valued, and desired commodity at your company. Take a look at the successful employees at any organization: Every single one is visible. If you fail to make yourself recognized at work, you run the risk that your peers and management may not actually know who you are, what work you're doing, the impact you are having on the company, or the overall value you bring to the organization. Increasing visibility is vital to success.

Exert Your Influence

Have impact and leverage your power to alter, change, and improve situations, regardless of your position or level of authority.

With influence, you move organizations forward and change outcomes for the better. You motivate, arouse interest, and sway others to do what is deemed important. You are depended on and seen as a difference maker who has the courage to make tough and important decisions. Without influence, your career stalls and comes to a standstill. You must have the courage to make an impact and be influential.

The following story emphasizes the impact that one person can have when perception, visibility, and influence are fully leveraged.

The Unknown Giant

Success means having the courage, the determination, and the will to become the person you believe you were meant to be.

—George Sheehan
American author and cardiologist

In 1944, cardiac surgery pioneer Dr. Alfred Blalock, renowned chief of surgery at Johns Hopkins University's medical school, was about to begin open-heart surgery on a 15-month-old baby who weighed only nine pounds. This operation, meant to fix the congenital heart defect called blue baby syndrome, had never before been performed on the heart. The medical establishment of the time deemed any operating on the heart to be off-limits, taboo, and essentially impossible.

Over 700 of the best doctors and researchers in the world were watching and waiting for this groundbreaking surgery to begin. Surprisingly, Dr. Blalock refused to initiate the process without one particular person present: He said that he must have his laboratory assistant, Vivien Thomas, at his side in order to commence surgery.

Racism and segregation were extremely rampant in Baltimore in the early 1940s. Vivien Thomas was African American. When he would wear his white lab coat, people were shocked. Typically, the only African American employees at Johns Hopkins University were janitors.

People were even *more* shocked when Dr. Blalock delayed the high-profile, controversial procedure to wait for Thomas to arrive and assist him. Blalock demanded that Vivien stand on a stool behind him to provide step-by-step instructions on performing the surgery.

Who Was Vivien Thomas?

Even in the face of such discrimination, Vivien Thomas was positively perceived and respected. Many people knew about his intelligence and skills, which allowed him to exert his influence completely. He earned this level of respect from Dr. Blalock, who initially hired him as a laboratory assistant—a low-paying job that Thomas took because he needed the money. Within five years, Thomas began to do the same work as postdoctoral researchers, though he continued to earn a janitor's wages.

Despite the fact that he had absolutely no medical training, Thomas worked 16 hours a day, performing hundreds of experimental surgeries on dogs in an effort to correct the condition that had come to be known as blue baby syndrome. In fact, Dr. Blalock was the one who had previously assisted Thomas during these operations on dogs. These hundreds of experiments gave Thomas much greater experience, which was precisely why Dr. Blalock needed him by his side when preparing for the 1944 breakthrough surgery, which actually led to curing the blue baby syndrome. In addition to guiding Dr. Blalock through blue baby surgeries, Thomas invented the instruments to perform the corrective heart surgery. These instruments are now commonplace in modern operating rooms.

The Legacy of Vivien Thomas

Vivien Thomas influenced generations of surgeons and lab technicians by teaching them operations that helped save thousands of lives. Dr. Blalock required all surgeons to learn surgical techniques from Thomas, techniques that eventually turned these surgeons into some of the most prominent medical doctors in the world.

Though the outside world did not perceive him as such, Thomas was an equal and a peer to the medical doctors with whom he worked. He didn't let his status or official job title as lab technician limit the ways he used his talents and skills. He stood out, got noticed, and became invaluable. *Despite his apparent lack of power and authority, Thomas became a difference maker who saved the lives of millions and changed the surgical profession forever. His influence became his legacy.*

Dr. Levi Watkins, the first African American cardiac resident and first African American chief resident in cardiac surgery at Johns Hopkins, said this about Vivien Thomas: "I think he is the most untalked about, unappreciated, unknown giant in the African American community. What he helped facilitate impacted people all over the world."[1] Dr. Watkins continued, "I think the implications are extraordinary. Take a man like this, without much formal anything, that impacts on inventions, and also impacts on the nation's premier heart surgeons. I look at him as a global person that rose above the conditions of his time."[2]

Vivien Thomas received an honorary doctorate from Johns Hopkins in 1971. After 37 years of altering people's perceptions, gaining worldwide visibility, and influencing the lives of millions, Thomas finally was recognized as a teacher and appointed to the medical school faculty.

Why This Book Is Important

You have to learn the rules of the game. And then you have to play better than anyone else.

—Albert Einstein
American (German-born) physicist and Nobel Prize winner

For over two decades, I have had firsthand experience working closely with thousands of executives, senior managers, directors, and employees at the world's leading companies. Before starting my own company, I lived and worked in London, Hong Kong, and San Francisco doing performance-improvement consulting for Ernst & Young in Hong Kong and change-management work at Andersen Consulting (now Accenture) in San Francisco. Since 1997, I've owned an executive coaching company that provides me access to clients from around the world and in countless industries.

This experience has provided me with a unique and expansive perspective on what both employees and employers want, need, and desire at work. No matter where my clients are from, what companies they work for, or what their titles or responsibilities are, I've seen a pattern in the kind of qualities that make one person more successful than another. I've learned that while everyone has access to perception, visibility, and influence, it's only the most successful leaders who fully utilize these elements.

Throughout this book, you'll be reading about what the best leaders have done to become renowned. As Seth Godin explains in his book *The Big Moo*, "Nothing is original. Most composers, great or not so great, are working with the same musical alphabet of pitches. It's putting the pitches together differently that creates something remarkable."[3] Even though everyone has access to perception, visibility, and influence, it's the combination of all three—the unique PVI model—that is the difference maker in leading you to extraordinary success.

Many of my clients protest that they're "too busy" to make the effort to bring perception, visibility, and influence into their work lives. They are consumed by and can barely keep up with their daily responsibilities. They oversee too many projects and have extensive to-do lists. They have seemingly endless meetings and are overwhelmed by e-mails. I'm guessing that many of your objections would sound the same. Well, let me ask: Do you think that leaders of large organizations receive fewer e-mails than you? Do they have fewer projects to work on, or shorter to-do lists? No. The difference is that they take time to prioritize perception, visibility, and influence. Despite the sense of urgency and importance that these demands provoke, these leaders still are able to make perception, visibility, and influence a vital part of their professional lives.

These well-known leaders understand the kind of time and effort that are necessary to make their top priority a reality; they appreciate the importance of improving their perception, increasing their visibility, and exerting their influence. As Henry Wadsworth Longfellow said, "The heights by great men reached and kept were not attained by sudden flight. But they, while their companions slept, were toiling upward in the night."

Focusing your attention on perception, visibility, and influence will have an immediate impact on your career. It will lead colleagues and managers alike to value and appreciate your contributions. You'll advance quickly while you gain recognition, enhanced responsibility, and increased respect.

Whom Is This Book For?

Show me an individual who does a good job and nothing else, and I'll show you an individual who will do the same good job almost forever.
                                                            —Lloyd G. Trotter
                        Former president and chief executive officer of GE Industrial

The Following People Will Benefit from This Book:
- New employees.
- Midlevel management.
- Upper management.
- Future company leaders.
- Minority employees.
- Managers providing this book to their employees.
- C-level (CEO, CFO, CIO, COO, CMO, etc.) leaders providing this book to their employees.

There are four attributes that directly contribute to your future success: *performance, perception, visibility,* and *influence.* Each of these four is weighted differently based on the point you're at in your career: a new employee, a midlevel manager, or in upper management.

This book's message focuses on three of the four attributes—perception, visibility, and influence. Performance is highlighted only in this section as a means of describing four time-specific career attributes. Of the four, performance is the one most often highlighted in books, journals, and other publications. No matter what position you are in, you must maintain a certain level of baseline performance to remain employable. Performing to the best of your ability is necessary at every level of your career. Developing perception, visibility, and influence, however, is an option and choice to which most professionals give little conscious attention. *Getting Ahead* is written specifically to bring your attention to the step-by-step PVI model that will ensure your future career success.

As you move from new employee to midlevel manager and ultimately to upper management, your focus on each of the four attributes for success will shift and change. The percentages listed for each in this section were revealed based on extensive research, including surveys and interviews with my executive coaching clients.

You might notice in the diagrams how performance dips extremely low (2 percent) in upper management. At this level, employees must be performing at the level required of them; otherwise, they never would have reached upper management. Thus, after reaching a certain level of career advancement, performance becomes a nondistinguishing skill.

New Employees

Performance is especially important when you're a new employee. You must quickly build a solid track record by doing your job exceptionally well and ensuring that all of your duties are fulfilled without issue. The chapters on perception are the most important area of focus for a new employee. You want to make the best impression and have others value your input. New employees also should concentrate on increasing their visibility; it allows you to quickly become known and respected. Important members of the company will take notice when a new employee's visibility reaches their level. This is also a time when you want to be aware of the *influencers*—the people in the organization who make the key decisions that impact others (see Table I.1 and Figure I.2).

TABLE I.1 New Employee Table

NEW EMPLOYEE	
ATTRIBUTE FOR SUCCESS	PERCENTAGE
Performance	51%
Perception	29%
Visibility	15%
Influence	5%

NEW EMPLOYEE

FIGURE I.2 New Employee Pie Chart

Midlevel Management

All three areas of PVI are important for the midlevel manager. You want to adjust others' perception of you so that they see you as someone who truly belongs in a senior-level position. You need the powerful and influential individuals in upper management to recognize, know, and respect you. You want to influence others by having them see you as a major player who can have a significant effect on the company. As you continue to excel at your job duties and responsibilities, others' expectations of you will shift. You'll be measured more by the impact you make on the overall organization, and less on what you can achieve through performance alone (see Table I.2 and Figure I.3).

TABLE I.2 Midlevel Management Table

MIDLEVEL MANAGEMENT	
ATTRIBUTE FOR SUCCESS	PERCENTAGE
Visibility	42%
Perception	30%
Influence	20%
Performance	8%

MIDLEVEL MANAGEMENT

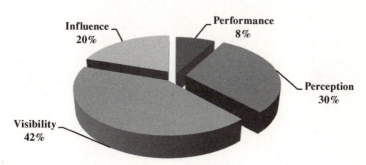

FIGURE I.3   Midlevel Management Pie Chart

Upper Management

The book's third section, on influence, is most relevant to members of upper management, though you will benefit from reviewing the sections on perception and visibility as well. As upper executives, you spend most of your time influencing significant results and people's behavior. By influencing others, you increase your value to the overall organization. Though it might sound counterintuitive, performance actually has an

almost minimal effect on your future career success. Although
your expertise allows you to maintain the perception and respect
you've established over the years, you must now perpetuate
the positive nature of that perception and shift it toward ever-
increasing respect. While visibility isn't as important as it used
to be, as a person in upper management, you still need to
make sure you have visibility to other executives who identify
you as someone who drives the company's success forward (see
Table I.3 and Figure I.4).

TABLE I.3   Upper Management Table

UPPER MANAGEMENT	
ATTRIBUTE FOR SUCCESS	PERCENTAGE
Influence	56%
Perception	25%
Visibility	17%
Performance	2%

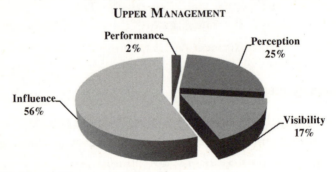

UPPER MANAGEMENT

FIGURE I.4   Upper Management Pie Chart

There are four other specific groups who will benefit
greatly from this book:

- **Future company leaders.** People in upper management are constantly on the lookout for fast-rising, high-potential employees. These are the up-and-coming stars—the organization's aspiring and emerging leaders. These talented employees need someone in upper management to recognize and mentor them as they develop PVI traits. To ensure the company's continued success, it's the responsibility of these upper-management employees to cultivate leaders and make sure they are learning the important aspects of PVI.

- **Minority employees.** As the number of minority employees within companies grows, management needs to reflect a similar level of diversity. A highly diversified management team is necessary to meet the company's needs. For example, women have been lacking leadership roles inside companies for decades. Now organizations are seeing women as a vital ingredient for future success. Minorities need a competitive advantage. PVI provides people with the necessary tools they need to compete and succeed.

- **Managers providing this book to their employees.** This book is an ideal tool for managers to gift to their employees. Employees need to focus on all three areas, with perception and visibility being the two most critical. Staff members want to make the right impression; they need advocates who are willing to tout their accomplishments and value to the company. PVI will help employees reveal themselves as effective players. Once they gain visibility, they can start to influence outcomes and compel others to see them as vital components of future management. Employees who fully leverage PVI become more valuable to a company, as their level of production and their overall contributions enhance the company's bottom-line performance.

- **C-level (CEO, CFO, CIO, COO, CMO, etc.) leaders providing this book to their employees.** We live in a time in which one employee can revolutionize a company or, for that matter, one start-up can revolutionize an entire industry. Employers have to recognize that they have hidden talent within their organizations. If they cannot unlock that talent and make it more visible, the company will underperform. They owe it to themselves to invest in these skills and to create a culture in which people are encouraged to lead and will be rewarded when they do. When employees build their perception, visibility, and influence, they are not just helping themselves; they are benefiting the entire company.

Stand Out from the Talent around You

A potential leader can hardly afford to wait to become a legend in his own time; to satisfy us, he must almost become a legend ahead of his time.

—Brock Brower
From "Where Have All the Leaders Gone?"
Life, October 8, 1971

You might think that you already understand the seemingly simple concepts of perception, visibility, and influence; they should not be too complicated to learn and understand. But this book is about more than learning and understanding these notions. Actually increasing your PVI at the level this book asks of you is a much more challenging concept. It's never easy to change the entrenched behaviors that undermine complete utilization of your PVI. This objective requires a certain level of action, commitment, and follow-through. I've seen my clients do what is necessary to propel themselves forward in their careers, and I know you can do the same.

By committing to improving your perception, visibility, and influence, you'll naturally begin to adopt new behaviors and habits. Neural pathways will be created as a rewiring of the brain occurs. As pioneer in leadership Warren Bennis said, "A person

does not gather learnings as pos-
sessions but rather becomes a
new person with those learnings
as part of his or her new self."[4]

> *Perception, visibility, and influence will help you stand out from the gifted group of stars that surrounds you.*

Therefore, you'll start to
notice new opportunities. You'll seek out ways to become
more visible. You'll take control of how others see you, and
make sure that it's an accurate reflection of your impact. You'll
identify opportunities to take initiative and show your worth
and value at work. You'll feel a renewal of fresh energy for
your career.

At a certain stage in your professional life, you'll be working
with the best. Everyone will be as good as or better than you. It
becomes more difficult to gain the recognition and promotions
you deserve. Chris Carmichael, Lance Armstrong's personal
coach and the U.S. Olympic Committee's Coach of the Year in
1999, advises, "You have to work hard and be smart to stand
out. You're no longer competing against just a handful of talented people; you're playing against people just like you who
were selected from a far greater candidate pool."[5] Perception,
visibility, and influence will help you stand out from the gifted
group of stars that surrounds you.

Gain the Competitive Advantage

If you don't have a competitive advantage, don't compete.
—Jack Welch
Former chairman and CEO of General Electric

As members of a technologically advanced society, our ability
to be faster, quicker, and smarter is challenged daily. Either you
keep up or you'll be run over. Many companies today function
within a cutthroat atmosphere in which employees either produce
results or are let go. You have to keep proving yourself and ensure
that others value your efforts and contributions. When you apply

perception, visibility, and influence, you gain the competitive edge necessary in today's intense and aggressive atmosphere.

Work is competitive. We operate in a global environment and are therefore forced to compete on a worldwide platform. If you want to stay ahead of the global competition, you must use each of the three areas of PVI fully. This book shows you how to do exactly that.

The fiercest competition you are likely to encounter will occur in the battle for promotions. You may work at a company where a bunch of executives (including your boss) sit around a table discussing whether you should receive a promotion. They talk about your character, your leadership qualities, the projects you manage, the people you oversee, the results you achieve, and your overall performance. Each manager tries to sell his or her candidate as the most deserving person for the promotion, while other members of the group will want to know why *you* deserve it. This environment is so competitive that you need to hone every asset you possibly can. Leveraging PVI will be the key to your success in scenarios like this one. It will help you to better compete with others and emerge victorious. Instead of worrying that a company can easily replace you, by implementing this PVI model, you will become irreplaceable.

Dedicating the necessary time and making PVI your top priority will give you the competitive advantage. You'll gain the most from all your efforts at work. You'll utilize your talents and reach your full potential. Increased productivity, performance, and job security will become commonplace.

Get the Most from Your Time at Work

If people knew how hard I had to work to gain my mastery, it would not seem so wonderful at all.

—Michelangelo
Italian painter, sculptor, architect, poet, and engineer

You spend one-third of your life—more than 100,000 hours—at work. To gain as much as possible from an endeavor to which you dedicate such a high percentage of your time, you must leverage PVI.

Employment represents a certain type of relationship in which both sides gain something from the other. Employees gain money, satisfaction, intellectual stimulation, connection, friendships, recognition, success, power, and more. Companies and employers gain increased profit, continued success, faster results, constant growth, sustainability, increased value, and constant productivity.

The problem with this exchange, however, is that employees can give *too* much of themselves. This occurs when your responsibilities increase, hours grow longer, you work harder, demands escalate, you become stressed out and overwhelmed, you miss spouse's and kids' events, and basically you have less time for anything but work.

PVI will help you gain more from your efforts and make the exchange between what you gain as an employee versus what your employer gains from you more equal. You'll be able to:

- Actively promote yourself as an asset and valuable person inside the organization.
- Increase your visibility to gain others' recognition and appreciation for your efforts.
- Be a person of influence who makes key decisions inside the organization.

Elevate Your PVI

We have to do the best we can. This is our sacred human responsibility.
—Albert Einstein
American (German-born) physicist and Nobel Prize winner

People resist working on PVI for a few reasons. For one thing, it's not a part of their job description, and they aren't sure what the exact value of their efforts will entail. Moreover, PVI might seem too confrontational and challenging. It extends beyond many individuals' comfort zones due to the amount of risk taking involved. It takes a lot of courage and confidence to create an ideal PVI state. If your job or next role needed an MBA, you would go to business school and work toward it. But working to increase PVI seems more daunting because it is less structured. This book gives PVI a structure. The vulnerability necessary to put oneself out there to be seen, to influence others, and to change people's opinions requires a tremendous amount of strength and persistence.

Despite the resistance many of us encounter—especially from ourselves—it's vital that each person dedicate extra time and effort to improving his or her PVI. You can't just sit back and do your job without placing the necessary energy and focus on this area. If you don't engage PVI, someone else will—and that person will pass you by and never look back. In his book *The 21 Indispensable Qualities of a Leader*, author John Maxwell shares a story that emphasizes the importance of PVI in developing your competitive advantage: "Former pro basketball player Bill Bradley attended a summer basketball camp at age fifteen conducted by 'Easy' Ed Macauley. During that camp, Macauley made a statement that changed Bradley's life: Just remember that if you're not working at your game to the utmost of your ability, there will be someone out there somewhere with equal ability. And one day you'll play each other, and he'll have the advantage. How do you measure up against that standard?"[6]

Make the commitment to implement as many of the ideas, concepts, tips, suggestions, and

> *The vulnerability necessary to put oneself out there to be seen, to influence others, and to change people's opinions requires a tremendous amount of strength and persistence.*

> *The one thing that's common to all successful people: They make a habit of doing things that unsuccessful people don't like to do.*
> —Michael Phelps

insights shared in this book as possible. Every step you take to elevate your PVI will make a substantial difference in your career success. You must put in the work and dedicate yourself to improving your PVI. Show the dedication that swimmer Michael Phelps had to in order to become the greatest Olympic champion ever, with 16 Olympic medals and a record eight gold medals at the Beijing 2008 Olympics. As Phelps said, ". . . the one thing that's common to all successful people: They make a habit of doing things that unsuccessful people don't like to do. . . . There are plenty of people with some amount of talent. Are you willing to go farther, work harder, be more committed and dedicated than anyone else? If others were inclined to take Sunday off, well, that just meant we might be one-seventh better. For five years, from 1998 to 2003, we did not believe in days off."[7]

It's this type of daily dedication and commitment to improving your PVI that is needed for you to escalate your career to the next level. This book will show you how. Let the journey begin.

> *The best journeys answer questions that, in the beginning, you didn't even think to ask.*
> —180° South

Part One

Improve Your Perception—Take Control
of How Others See You

1

Power of Perception

There is no truth. There is only perception.

—Gustave Flaubert
French writer, author of *Madame Bovary*

How Do You Want to Be Known?

One morning in 1888, a man wakes up and goes outside to retrieve his newspaper. He returns to his home and sits down in his favorite chair as he does every day. He begins reading the newspaper and quickly turns to the obituary section. The man's brother has just died, and he wants to read what was said about him. In the obituary section, he is struck by the large headline: "The merchant of death is dead." He continues reading. The article tells of a merchant who became "rich by finding ways to kill more people faster than ever before." He finishes reading the obituary, closes the newspaper, and sits in shock. He is speechless and doesn't move. The obituary is supposed to be about his brother, but it was mistakenly written about him. He is alive—not dead—reading his own obituary.[1]

This man, the inventor of dynamite, certainly doesn't want to be remembered as a "merchant of death." He decides to take his fortune and use it to establish awards for accomplishments in various fields that benefit humanity. These awards are eventually granted to such famous people as Dr. Martin Luther King Jr., Mother Teresa, the Dalai Lama, and Nelson Mandela.

The person who established these awards, including the Nobel Peace Prize, was Dr. Alfred Nobel. He is remembered today for establishing the Nobel Prizes—not for his explosive inventions. Though Dr. Nobel was initially perceived one way, he was able to completely change the perception people had of him and ensure that he was remembered in a positive light.

The Power of Perception

Leadership is a performance. You have to be conscious about your behavior, because everyone else is.

—Carly Fiorina
Former chairman and chief executive officer
of Hewlett-Packard Company

You are being perceived, either positively or negatively, every day of your work (and personal) life. Others are constantly viewing and making judgments of you. The impact of this perception can happen quickly; it takes only a few seconds to form an opinion. Even though you don't have control of how others view you, you do have control over your actions, which can substantially affect others' perceptions. David Sokol, chairman of the board of MidAmerican Energy Holdings Company, said, "My father taught me that it is difficult to control others' perceptions, but I can always control my own actions, and these actions can, over time, alter those perceptions."[2]

While this book focuses on how you can take *some* control of how others see you, it's important to note that there *is* a limit to the amount of control you have. In other words, you can do only so much. You can't influence someone's perception 100 percent of the time. Recognizing this limitation helps you accept the circumstances when you encounter people who sim-

> *Proactively shaping others' perceptions of you is a key strategy for standing out, gaining credit for your work, and, ultimately, achieving career advancement.*

ply won't change their perceptions of you. Though unchangeable situations like these are rare, it is necessary to mention them. This entire section is focused on others' beliefs about you, and how you can beneficially alter them.

The power of perception is important because it completely determines how people view you, and, therefore, how they act toward and around you. Their opinion can be positive or negative. If it's negative, it can undermine your career. You'll have to work even harder to make sure people appreciate your value and notice your overall impact. If it's positive, it can enhance your career and make it easier for you to attain what you want. Either way, you want to influence perception so that you are being seen as you want to be seen. When you can alter people's opinions to benefit yourself—by compelling others to see you as a valuable and impactful person at work—you will gain respect and influence. Proactively shaping others' perceptions of you is a key strategy for standing out, gaining credit for your work, and, ultimately, achieving career advancement.

Just as Dr. Alfred Nobel showed that he could make a choice—one that not many people would have made—to change others' opinions of him, you too can make choices that will positively affect perception. You want people to see you as the talented, smart, effective employee that you are. To be viewed as anything less would be a disservice to you and to all the effort that you put into your job. Having people on your side recognizing your talents and your worth will greatly enhance their appreciation for what you do.

What Is Perception?

It's not what you look at that matters.
It's what others see.

—Henry David Thoreau
American author and poet, best known for his work *Walden*

Perception is what someone notices, sees, or is aware of. When you perceive, you often unconsciously observe what is happening without being consciously aware of the content that's forming in your mind. The author of an article titled "Unwritten Rules: What You Don't Know Can Hurt Your Career," Laura Sabattini, PhD, says, "Employees learn not only by observing individual behaviors, but also by noting how people interact with one another, dress, and communicate verbally and nonverbally (for example, through body language but also via e-mail and at meetings)."[3] You often form opinions when you have preconceived ideas about a topic or person you're observing, even if what you observe isn't real or true. Perception takes the prior knowledge you already have and filters your observations through this lens.

So how *do* others see and create an opinion of you? Perception is affected by a variety of factors, including:

- What people notice about you.
- The behaviors that make an impression.
- The image you have.
- The attitudes you project.
- The opinions you hold.

I have chosen to not address how appearance (clothing, grooming, style, etc.) affects perception and image, as there are many books already devoted to the subject. While it's certainly important, it's not an aspect of perception discussed in this book.

Beware of Ego Vision

You need to be honest with yourself about who you are before you can focus on the way you want others to perceive you. Everyone wants the promotion when the opportunity comes along. However, most of us fail to see that we may not be performing strongly enough in the areas that we need to excel in to receive a promotion. One client of mine who works at one of the largest design firms in the world said, "I have had people who think that because they can design a bathroom, they're ready to lead a design team for an expansion of a 150,000-square-foot addition to a mall."

You can begin by conducting a candid assessment of your true skill level. By comparing the way that others perceive you with your genuine skill level, you can determine whether your current ability corresponds to where you want to go. This is essentially about getting to the next stage, and to do that, you must be able to assess yourself—and your skill level—correctly. Though you might believe that you're ready for advancement, you may not be evaluating your skill level accurately. You need to figure out what abilities are needed at the next level and discern whether you have them before you even consider the next step.

People can't exert influence if their own perception of who they are is delusional. Before embarking on the next step, you have to ask, "Based on my current skills, am I ready to take on the next level?"

How Does Perception Work?

The reality of life is that your perceptions—right or wrong—influence everything else you do. When you get a proper perspective of your perceptions, you may be surprised how many other things fall into place.
—Roger Birkman
American psychologist and expert on behavioral assessment

Where does perception begin, and how does it progress into forming an actual opinion about something? Perception always starts with an observation that ultimately becomes cemented in your mind as the truth. The perception process includes eight levels that the mind goes through to create an ultimate and unwavering perception that you believe is your reality (see Figure 1.1).

The first step in the perception process is to *observe* something, such as a person, event, or situation. The step following this initial observation is to make an *assessment* of what you have observed, which involves reviewing and trying to understand it. After assessment, the formation of an *opinion* occurs. This entails the need to contemplate information that the mind collects. Opinion leads directly to the tendency to make a *judgment* based on the feelings, thoughts, and opinions developed. The moment a judgment becomes active in your mind, you have initiated the process of *perception*.

Once perception has started, the *reality* of what you see begins to take effect. This provides a level of certainty. Once the perception becomes the reality, the person begins to think that this is what he or she actually *believes*, and develops faith and confidence in this belief. The final step occurs when one

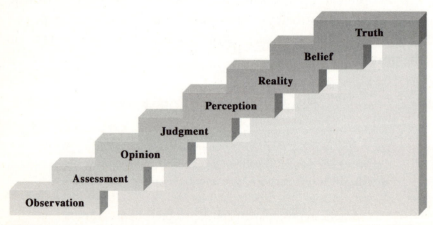

FIGURE 1.1   The Perception Process

considers the perception to be *truth*. The truth provides such certainty for a person that it makes it difficult to change or alter the perception that one has created.

By understanding these eight levels, you'll be equipped with the necessary awareness to challenge the perceptions people have of you. Further, you will resist forming unfounded opinions and judgments of others.

In an article titled "Perception Matters," Mike Myatt, managing director of coaching and leadership firm N2growth, took the expression "seeing the glass half empty or half full" and expanded the number of people who could view the same glass in many different ways.

It is quite clear reviewing the 11 different viewpoints that everyone can view the same situation differently. These are excellent examples of how perception changes based on each person. Someone's disposition, prior experience, and background directly impact how one views others. As you can see, 11 vastly different observations are created by answering the simple question, "Is the glass half empty or half full?"

1. **The Optimist:** The glass is half full.
2. **The Pessimist:** The glass is half empty.
3. **The Salesperson:** How much water would you like your glass to hold?
4. **The Accountant:** Does the glass really need all that water?
5. **The Attorney:** If there are enough people on one side of this issue I can file a class action suit.
6. **The Investment Banker:** I'm only 50 percent leveraged.
7. **The Engineer:** The glass is twice as big as it needs to be.
8. **The Quantum Physicist:** The glass has a 50 percent probability of holding water.
9. **The Philosopher:** If nobody looks at the glass, who's to say whether it's half full or half empty?
10. **The Politician:** Let's take a poll and then I'll render my opinion as to how full or empty the glass is.
11. **The Servant Leader:** Whatever the amount of water, I'll use it first to quench the thirst of those I lead.[4]

These 11 statements illustrate the fact that others constantly perceive you in a variety of ways, based on their own outlooks, attitudes, and backgrounds. Now imagine what it's like when you move beyond the simple subject of viewing a glass of water and take it to the most complicated living creatures in the world—human beings. Every person has his or her own unique way of viewing you. The more fully you can understand this concept and recognize the numerous ways in which you might be perceived, the greater control you will have over how that perception impacts how others view you. Without this knowledge, you allow people to develop their own (usually false) perceptions of you, founded through their own history and influence. When you understand how one seemingly straightforward situation can be viewed a million different ways, you begin to see the power of how perception affects others' opinions of you.

Why Is Perception Important?

It takes 20 years to build a reputation and five minutes to ruin it. If you think about that, you'll do things differently.

—Warren Buffett
American investor, industrialist, and philanthropist

Everything you do on a daily basis is being observed and documented inside the brains of every single person with whom you come into contact. These interactions can be extensive (for example, having conversations with your boss or employee) or limited (for example, copying someone on an e-mail). In either case, everyone has an opinion of you that directly affects your ability to be promoted, receive assignments you want, get a raise or bonus, and more.

Everything you do is being remembered by someone.

Everything you do is being remembered by someone. This is why perception is important. Case in point: A senior director at Procter & Gamble recently contacted me for coaching. He had spent three months focusing on improving the perception others had of him so that he could win a promotion when the next promotion cycle came around. When the time came, someone else was chosen instead of him. This was when our work began.

I told him during one of our coaching sessions, "Imagine that all of your colleagues have been watching everything you've been doing for five years. Although your actions have made an impression on them, they aren't even aware of this impression. It's not until they are asked during the promotion cycle, 'Do you think that *this senior director* deserves a promotion?' that they will call up all the unconscious situations, circumstances, observations, evaluations, and opinions they have generated in the five years of interacting with you." The truth of this statement surprised him, and he immediately knew it to be accurate. My client realized how the perception others had of him during the previous years had negatively determined the immediate promotion cycle for which he had spent only a few months preparing.

Perceptions clearly have a substantial impact on your career. Once formed, they are difficult to change, and attempting to do so can take a long time. An article titled "Shape Perceptions of Your Work, Early and Often" points out: "Perceptions are also self-sustaining because, once people have formed an impression of another, they stop actively gathering new information." In other words, once I have decided that you are smart, I won't pay as much attention to every little thing you do, which means you can more easily get away with being not so brilliant without my noticing.[5]

People will rely on the perception they have of you rather than the actual work, accomplishments, and value you've contributed. As I clearly conveyed in the case with my client, the past five years of perception are more important in determining whether you are promoted than are the three months (or even days) during which you hastily prepare before your performance review or next promotion cycle.

The Benefits of Perception Management

You are only as wise as others perceive you to be.

—M. Shawn Cole

Ensuring that you create the right impression inside your company will enable you to greatly benefit your career. The following describes the advantages of managing perception.

Impact Your Career Advancement

How quickly and successfully you advance in a company is a result of the perception you create, not just the merit you have accumulated or the skill level you have achieved.

Example: A senior business development manager who worked for Cisco Systems for 11 years contacted me for coaching because he wasn't advancing up the corporate ladder as quickly as he wanted to. Even though he had solid performance reviews and excellent job skills, he had gone four years without a promotion.

This man's attitude was that his work should speak for itself, and that he didn't need to do anything to help improve perception. By operating under this mind-set, he did very little to increase his exposure or visibility with senior management. Thus, executives at his company didn't know how valuable he was to the organization, which negated any opportunities for career advancement.

Keep Your Status as a Desired Employee Inside the Company

You can't rely solely on skill, merit, and hard work for employability and career success. You realize at some point in your career

*that your continued achievement at a given company is based on
perception.*

Example: Two employees, both accountants but at two different firms (Ernst & Young and KPMG), came out of college
and worked at their respective companies the same amount of
time. They put in long hours, worked hard, and had similar skill
sets. They both had nearly identical career success. On paper,
they seemed to be very similar. However, one got laid off and
the other one didn't. Why would this happen? Discussing the
situation further, the two friends realized that one had created
a better perception in his organization than the other had.
Even though they both worked hard and developed first-rate
skills, one had earned a reputa-
tion of not being much of a
team player. This was all it
took for the person to be laid off.

> *You can't rely solely on skill, merit,
> and hard work for employability and
> career success.*

Perception is important; it can directly affect whether you
are a desired employee. If an organization doesn't find you
desirable, then you lose employability.

Eliminate the Negative Ways Others May See You

*Others can view your behavior and attitude negatively. They may dis-
like you or look unfavorably on something you do. You want to eliminate these damaging perceptions and take actions that cause others to
see you in a more positive light.*

Example: Five people attend a regular weekly business
meeting. Each has some personality trait that others might view
negatively. One person talks too much; another doesn't listen
well; the third person is quiet and doesn't speak up very often;
the fourth is outspoken and assertive with her opinions; and the
fifth person acts like a know-it-all, coming across as arrogant
and condescending.

None of these people have any idea that they're exhibiting a
behavior that someone else dislikes. The key to eliminating
these habits is to begin to notice how your behavior affects

others. For example, when you speak up, do others begin to lose interest, look away, make faces, or become agitated? Observing others' reactions to you is the first step to becoming aware of the very actions that others find objectionable and then to being able to change them.

Reduce the Number of Career-Limiting Maneuvers

While it may take only a few moments to do something that others perceive critically, it becomes a career-limiting move and can impair you professionally for a long time to come.

Example: An employee and his manager were e-mailing each other back and forth about how to handle an issue with a client, and were both being honest about this client's particularly difficult personality. Some of these remarks were disparaging. When the manager provided, via e-mail, a detailed solution to resolve the issue, the employee decided to forward this e-mail to the client. However, the employee also accidentally included the electronic trail of disparaging private comments the manager had thought to be making in confidence. The client took offense to what was said in the e-mail and pulled the account from the firm.

Imagine that you were the manager in this scenario. You would have judgments and a strong opinion about the employee who made this error. You might judge the employee as careless, and most likely you would be hesitant to trust him again. It might take months or even years to restore this confidence.

Protect Your Online Public Image

The world is nothing but my perception of it.
I see only through myself. I hear only through the filter of my story.
—Byron Katie
American speaker and author, specializing in self-inquiry

The online world has added yet another dimension to the importance of perception. The World Wide Web was nonexistent 20 years ago, but its impact today has huge ramifications for your image. In 2010, the Nielsen Company produced a report about the effect of social media, which found that 75 percent of U.S. households (and 74 percent globally) visit a social networking site regularly. In short, three out of four people with whom you interact are engaging in social networking.[6]

Every online social networking site (for example, LinkedIn, Facebook, Twitter, and MySpace) is out there for anyone to view. For that reason, you need to be aware of how you are portraying yourself in this public way. Whatever you do can be viewed by your company and directly affect how others perceive you. This is why it's best to separate your private life from your professional life whenever possible.

If you choose to display information on your social networking sites publicly, be aware that you always are connected to and representing the company for which you work. Its brand and image are extremely important to it. You must take care not to say anything negative online about your job, boss, coworkers, salary, lack of raises, and so on, because everything you say directly reflects on your company. People have been fired because of statements they posted on social networking sites. You also want to be careful about posting pictures from parties, vacations, or other personal events that portray you unfavorably or unintentionally reveal information about you. A client of mine told me once that his coworker had called in sick on Halloween. The following week, however, her boss saw pictures of her on Facebook in costume, looking quite well.

This is especially true if you are (or are about to be) looking for employment. Remember that employers don't just use online search engines to research job candidates. They rely more and more on social networking. In fact, a study conducted by employment search engine CareerBuilder.com found that nearly half of employers use social networking sites to research potential job candidates. Information technology companies are especially likely to screen candidates this way; two-thirds of tech companies surveyed scour sites such as Facebook, LinkedIn, and MySpace to gather an up-close, behind-the-scenes look at candidates they can't determine from merely interviewing or reading résumés. So if you're in the job market—or may be in the future—be aware of what you put out on the Internet. If it's out there—good or bad—it's just a mouse click away from a hiring manager. And the results can be catastrophic. CareerBuilder .com's survey revealed that one in three employers found content that caused them *not* to hire a candidate.

It can feel as if you are just writing in your journal when you are on these social networking sites, and you might assume that only your friends (outside of work) will read them. It's easy to forget how vast is the network of people who can read what you write. You must always remain aware of how you are portraying yourself.

Here are a few tips to ensure that others perceive you positively online:

- Search your name on the Internet to see what content is on the Web.
- Check out other major social networks to assess whether you have made the impression you want to make.
- Identify the Web pages where you have posted information about yourself (including your résumé or other work-related items) and make sure they are up-to-date and positively reflect you.
- Remove any negative content.
- Provocative or inappropriate photographs or information top the list of red flags to employers. When in doubt, take it out.
- Create favorable content about yourself and try to make it appear as high as possible in search results.

- Use privacy settings so that your personal information and photos aren't viewable by the public.
- Write and submit well-researched, articulate letters to the editors of the top trade publications in your industry. Focus on current, relevant issues.
- Purchase your name as a domain name and create an active website that makes the best impression possible.
- Post on free publisher websites articles that you've written that convey your expertise.
- Write comments on other blogs that show your level of intelligence and expertise.
- Create a blog and write quality content for it.

The perception you create at work can be directly influenced by what you publicize on your social networking sites. Review all of these sites immediately, and remove anything that portrays you in a negative or unfavorable light.

I provide a summary of the key points and specific action steps at the end of each chapter. By implementing each of these ideas, you'll fulfill your PVI potential and reach your deserved next level.

Summary and Action Steps

Chapter 2 discusses the seven different influencers that directly affect and alter perception. Before we deal with these topics, let's review the material from Chapter 1 and see what actions you can take based on what has been covered.

Summary

- *Perception occurs on a daily basis.* Other people are constantly observing and forming opinions of you. Even though

perception directly affects how people view you, you do
have control over your actions, which can alter perceptions.

- *Understand the eight levels of perception* (see Figure 1.1).
  Perception starts with an *observation* and ends with someone
  believing this perception as the *truth*.

- *Perception can directly affect your career advancement.* Perception helps you remain employable and reduces the number
  of career-limiting moves. Using your perception to your
  benefit eliminates the negative ways others might view you,
  and continues to enhance your level of desirability.

- *Online social networking affects perception.* If not monitored
  correctly, social networking can negatively affect the way
  members of your company perceive you. What you say and
  post is out there for public view, so it's important to be
  aware of how you portray yourself.

Take Action Now

- Consider how others perceive you in your company, both
  positively and negatively. Review the section "What Is
  Perception?" to help you generate ideas and information.
  Schedule with yourself a 30-minute self-reflection session
  that provides you the time to write out a description of how
  you are perceived.

- Conduct an assessment of your skill level wherein you honestly analyze your skills in terms of where you are versus
  where you want to be—and what you need to do to close
  this gap. Make two lists: one with the current abilities you
  possess, and a second one that identifies the skills needed at
  the next level. Compare the two and discern where you
  need to focus your improvement efforts right now.

- Review the section on "The Benefits of Perception Management" and select which one most resonates with you. Have
  you ever found yourself in a situation similar to any of

these—as either the person being perceived or the one seeing someone else in a certain light?

- Review all of your social networking sites from two perspectives. First, make sure you portray yourself as you want to be perceived. Second, make sure you represent your company's image appropriately.

2

Seven Influencers on Perception

What we perceive and understand depends upon what we are.
—Aldous Huxley
English writer, author of *Brave New World*

O ther people's perception is influenced by a variety of factors that are out of your control. Whether it's the environment in which you grew up, the culture of which you have been a part, your personality, your life experiences, or your family's influence—all of these areas can affect how your colleagues and managers perceive you.

Figure 2.1 displays the seven most common influencers on perception. I have compiled these elements during 15 years of extensive research gathered while working with and interviewing coaching clients from a variety of cultures around the world.

1. Cultural Background

Diverse cultural differences exist around the world. An individual's cultural background directly influences how he or she

FIGURE 2.1   The Seven Influencers on Perception

behaves at work. In turn, this influence can affect the perception others develop.

Examples: A person from India works in an American technology company. He has been raised and taught not to speak up, stand out, bring attention to himself, or become too visible.

A coworker from Japan may appear to be agreeable even though he doesn't like what he is hearing, because he was taught in his native culture that it is impolite to say no, create conflict, or provide resistance.

Impact: These two people must struggle to make themselves visible because not enough people of influence know about their accomplishments. A lot of their hard work and value are going unnoticed. These people feel falsely perceived, especially because the perceptions others have do not match the actual impact they are making on the company.

What Can You Do?

- *Seek out projects or assignments with visibility.* Talk to your boss to see whether you can be assigned to projects that have the high-level visibility you desire. Once you begin working on a project, make sure that the influential players know who you are. Focus on how your actions affect the bottom line of the company.

- *Share your accomplishments.* Inform others, especially those with influence, of the work you are actually doing and how it financially impacts the organization. Others need to hear about your accomplishments from *you*. If they don't, they can only operate from limited perception and secondhand information. We discuss more ways to share your accomplishments in Chapter 5 (on self-promotion).

- *Customize your management style to each employee.* Identify each of your employees' different cultural and regional backgrounds. Spend some time learning about these various cultures so that you can customize your management style to best interact with each individual.

2. Personality Traits

Each person has unique qualities that shed light on his or her personality. Your individuality can show up in diverse and distinctive ways, and is likely to affect how others perceive you. The various types of personalities might be as diverse as talkative, upbeat, friendly, aggressive, shy, considerate, organized, dependable, unkind, intellectual, reserved, funny—and countless others. Some might consider you to be introverted or extraverted, to have an optimistic or cynical attitude, to be proactive or passive, to be open-minded or closed-minded, to take initiative or wait for direction, to be self-reliant or too dependent on others, to be patient or impatient, to be indecisive or decisive, to be driven or lazy, to like being around people or prefer to work alone, and so forth.

Examples: You are extraverted and proactive. People like you and are drawn to you. You are productive, achieve results, and are seen by colleagues as a team player.

You are shy, hesitant, and passive. You focus on accomplishing all the work that needs to be done. You limit your interaction with others because you feel that it distracts you from your tasks.

Impact: Since your dominant personality traits create certain perceptions, the key is to recognize the ways in which your personality traits influence how others see you. People exhibit their characteristics without appreciating the effect they have on others. Although you are just being yourself, this can mar—or enhance—others' views of you.

What Can You Do?

- *Identify your dominant personality traits.* Come up with the three personality traits that most significantly define your character. Choose two or three people with whom you work regularly and notice how your personality positively or negatively influences how they see you.

- *Choose one personality trait to improve.* Select the personality trait that you've realized needs the most improvement. Next, identify two actions you can take to improve this specific trait. For example, if you are typically quiet during meetings, commit to speaking up at your next meeting. Prepare by having two specific ideas ready to share.

- *Know your employees' most significant traits.* Discover each of your employees' most dominant personality traits. Discuss how these traits affect others' perceptions of them during your next one-on-one meeting.

3. Your Family of Origin

The family environment in which you grew up, the dominant qualities that characterize your family, and the kind of messages you consistently heard during your childhood directly affect how you will interact with others at work.

Examples: People will react differently to similar situations if they came from:

- A family that consistently showed disrespect for one another and engaged in name-calling, criticism, and fighting.
- A family that was supportive, loving, and communicative.
- A family that was authoritative, disciplined, and rigid.
- A family that was hands-off and isolated.

Familial statements can negatively influence your behavior. For instance, you might have constantly heard these statements:

- "Be a good girl and don't speak up."
- "Don't bring too much attention to yourself."
- "Just work hard and be quiet."
- "Stand up for yourself and don't let anyone walk over you."
- "Speak up and make sure you are heard."

Impact: The type of guidance you received from your parents can have an effect on how you behave at work. If you are used to criticism and name-calling, you might be a boss who is extra critical of others. You might never praise others and be difficult to please. On the other end of the spectrum, if you grew up in an open and cooperative environment, you will probably tend to make sure you communicate clearly and check to see that others understand you. If you are disciplined and rigid, you will run a tight ship and make certain everyone follows the rules.

What Can You Do?

- *Learn the types of qualities that dominated your family.* To better understand yourself, think about the other members and general mind-set of the family environment in which you were raised. Becoming aware of your family dynamics will shed light on how you behave as a leader, a manager, and an employee.

- *Identify the top three messages you heard growing up.* Think about the statements you constantly heard when you were younger, and make sure you identify to which parent you attribute each statement. Notice how often you mimic these statements and how they affect your daily professional behavior.
- *Understand the family dynamics in which your employees were raised.* Spend time getting to know your employees. Leave the office environment, go to lunch, and share time with them. Find ways to connect with them on a nonprofessional level. These types of nonoffice environments are much more conducive to learning about a person's family dynamics. The more you understand what type of families your employees come from, the easier it will be to manage them.

4. Regional Differences

Though it's certainly not set in stone, some people might act differently based on where they grew up or where they currently live. Whether it's one of the various U.S. states or another country entirely, your place of origin can significantly influence who you are and how others perceive you. Many of these examples may appear to be stereotypical; however, they do represent some oft-encountered attitudes and patterns.

Examples:

- A New Yorker may tend to be aggressive and direct.
- A Southerner might be more polite and reticent.
- A Californian is laid-back.
- British (UK) people often are reserved and private.
- Australians are outgoing and friendly, and enjoy socializing.

Impact: People tend to make judgments based on where you are from—even though that's not your desire. The New Yorker's background might cause someone who isn't used to assertive behavior to make an unfavorable judgment about the kind of person she is, even when the perception is wrong. This tendency might lead someone to a positive perception of the Southerner, assuming that he is very easy to get along with. At the same time, this individual might be *too* nice, and just let things happen without taking a stand against behaviors that undermine his authority. Last, the Californian might be viewed as lazy, not interested, or unengaged—an unflattering perception that could lessen others' desire to work with this individual.

What Can You Do?

- *Know where the people you interact with grew up.* Do research and learn about the home area of people with whom you work, and make sure you understand the traits and behaviors associated with the people from this region or country. Getting an idea about the type of area from which they originate will allow you to understand them better. If other people feel that you identify with them, they will perceive you more positively.

- *Adjust your behavior.* Consider the opinions that people might hold—based on stereotypes or actual experiences—about your own place of origin. Identify any behaviors associated with this that others might view negatively. Then try to adjust these behaviors enough so that they don't contribute to—or cause others to form—a disparaging impression of you.

- *Identify the regional differences of each direct report.* Spend time with all of your direct reports to learn about their locations of origin. After developing an understanding of their regional backgrounds, schedule one-on-one meetings to delve into this further. Share with them specific examples of how their region can positively and negatively affect how others perceive them.

5. Challenges for Women

Though women make up nearly half of the workforce (48 percent), they hold only 20 percent of top management positions. Much research has proven that men receive more promotions than women. The inequality that exists within the workplace affects how women are perceived inside the organization.

Examples: A woman attends meetings and is surrounded predominantly by men. The fact that she is the only female present affects how everyone else perceives her.

A woman tries to speak at the same time as her male coworker. If she doesn't make her statement as strongly as her male counterpart, the boss present at the meeting often will choose to hear what the male coworker has to say first.

Impact: Women are easily judged because they are the minority. The dominant male energy can make females feel less included. They may be intimidated by this inequality, and may in turn become uncomfortable. They might even feel defeated and unnoticed.

What Can You Do?

- *Find a male mentor.* A male mentor can provide insight on how to work in a predominantly male environment.
- *Create advocates.* Developing a relationship with one or two advocates within a group of male colleagues will provide valuable support. These advocates can speak up on your behalf and support you when you bring solutions and ideas forward. They will also defend you from anyone who might try to undermine your efforts. If you are an employer, it might be a good idea to implement and oversee these kinds of advocacy and mentoring programs at your office.
- *Recognize the challenges women employees face.* Whether you are a male or female manager, take extra care to become aware of the difficulties women employees might be facing.

Ask women employees directly what challenges they have being the minority at work (for example, being treated unfairly, going unnoticed, not being included, or being defeated, judged, or not fully respected). Create an action plan with them to help alleviate the difficulties.

6. Varied Levels of Social Skills

When you are comfortable communicating socially and interacting with others, members of your organization will perceive you more advantageously. Well-developed social skills will help you be successful and interact with influential people who then view you in a more positive light.

Examples: The following are some indications that you are proficient at interacting socially:

- You know what to say at the right time.
- You are comfortable approaching people you don't know and talking with them.
- You don't feel anxiety when speaking and interacting with others.
- You feel at ease sharing information about yourself with others.
- You convey confident body language (direct eye contact, upright posture, strong vocal tone, and expressive hand gestures when talking).
- You share information in a way that's easy for others to comprehend.

Impact: Your social skills are one of the most powerful ways to directly affect others' opinions of you. People are quick to judge others based on their ability to converse comfortably, share information about themselves, and put people at ease.

Displaying poor social skills might keep others from seeing who you really are and recognizing your talents and skills.

What Can You Do?

- *Learn from others.* Find two people you know who have excellent social skills. Observe them and watch what they effortlessly do. These are skills that you can learn and cultivate. Ask them for guidance to ascertain the tools necessary to improve your social skills.
- *Buy a social skills book.* Read a book or two on the art of social skills. The authors of these books are experts who have detailed processes and important insights on how to improve these abilities. By applying these tips, you can improve your social skills dramatically.
- *Improve your subordinates' social skills.* Identify the employees who lack well-developed social skills. Choose two areas in which they need to improve and discuss what steps they should take. Inform them of the benefits of enhancing their mannerisms when interacting with others and how doing so will affect people's opinions of them.

7. Friends at Work

The coworkers you seek out and interact with during breaks, at lunch, and outside of the office are your friends at work. These individuals directly affect the perception others have of you.

Examples:

- You are a manager inside a medium-size organization and are close friends with the CEO.
- You spend a lot of time with someone who isn't respected and whom no one in the organization likes.
- You are close friends with a boss who is well liked and highly regarded.

- You interact with someone who gossips all the time and talks negatively about people.

Impact: The reputation of the coworkers with whom you interact reflects on you. Ideally, you can be friends with anyone you choose; however, those connections have implications. The degree to which the people you associate with are or are not respected affects how others view you.

What Can You Do?

- *Identify the five people with whom you spend the most time at work.* Write down next to each person's name how that person is perceived, negatively or positively, in the organization. Try to spend time with people who will enhance your reputation, not mar it. If it is important for you to remain friends with someone who is perceived unfavorably, then you might want to try, for the benefit of you both, to help that person improve his or her reputation.
- *Choose the two most influential people at your place of work.* These two people are the ones with whom you want to spend time. The more you associate with people who are respected in the company, the greater the respect that will rub off on you.
- *Make introductions for your employees.* As a manager, review your employees and identify who lacks strong connections with highly regarded individuals. Find opportunities to make introductions to solid and reputable people for these employees.

Summary and Action Steps

The following are the Chapter 2 summary and action steps. Next, we'll move on to Chapter 3, which will introduce a four-step process to help you change and create the right perception.

Summary

- *There are seven different factors that directly affect how others perceive you:*
  1. Cultural differences.
  2. Personality traits.
  3. The type of family in which you grew up.
  4. The location of your upbringing (as well as where you currently live).
  5. The challenges that women face in the workplace.
  6. The level of social skills you display.
  7. The friends with whom you engage and spend time.
- *Each of these seven factors is operating all the time, mostly on unconscious levels.* The more you notice recurring patterns, the easier it will be to change them. Your ability to alter each of these factors will influence how others view you and turn perception into an asset that enhances your career.

Take Action Now

- Recall specific situations or examples that involved each of the seven factors. You can focus either on how your perception of others was influenced or on how you were affected by others' perceptions of you. Recalling these scenarios will help you notice how prevalent these judgments are and how easy they are to make.
- Review each of the seven different areas that affect perception, and choose one action to implement from each of the seven areas. Review the "What Can You Do?" sections for specific ideas.

3

The Four-Step Perception Management Process

Perception is real even when it is not reality.

—Edward de Bono
Physician, author, and originator of the term *lateral thinking*

Creating the ideal perception entails taking four steps, each of which will help you enhance the current view others have of you and improve any negative opinions that exist (see Figure 3.1). The first step is to discern how you *think* you are perceived. Each and every behavior you exhibit at work is being observed and directly affects how others view you. Inaccurate perceptions show you how easy it is for others to incorrectly perceive you.

The second step is to know how you *actually* are perceived, which you can accomplish by asking for feedback from others. The third step focuses on determining how you *want* to be perceived. Here, you'll create the ideal perception and image. In the fourth step, you'll learn how to *change* perception so it reflects who you are.

The four steps are as follows:

Step 1—How you ***think*** you are perceived.

Step 2—How you ***actually*** are perceived.

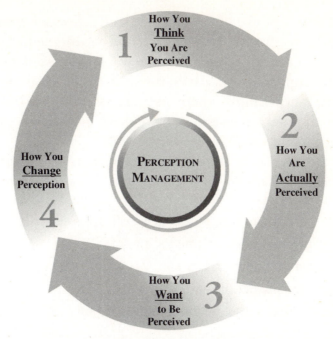

FIGURE 3.1   The Four-Step Perception Management Process

Step 3—How you *want* to be perceived.

Step 4—How you *change* perception.

Step 1: How You *Think* You Are Perceived

Many people don't know how they are perceived at work. They have given little thought to how others view them. This is surprising because, in most cases, people automatically size up an individual and immediately create opinions seconds after meeting someone. This initial information makes an impression and often cements a lasting perception.

One way to appreciate the power of perception is to understand how first impressions can be so influential. Our tendency is to form an immediate opinion of someone when we first meet him or her. An article from *Psychology Today* reinforces this point: "Consider one study in which untrained subjects were shown 20- to 32-second videotaped segments of job applicants greeting interviewers. The subjects then rated the applicants on attributes such as self-assurance and likability. Surprisingly, their assessments were very close to those of trained interviewers who spent at least 20 minutes with each applicant."[1]

Recall what your initial thoughts were when you first met someone—for example, your impressions of someone when:

- You started working with a new colleague at work.
- You interviewed someone for a job.
- You went on a first date.
- You met new people at a party.
- You worked with a new colleague on a project.
- You met with a new boss.
- You introduced yourself to a new neighbor.

Some of these examples might have recently occurred. Once you form an opinion, it most often integrates into a long-lasting perception of someone. The important point is that you aren't the only one establishing opinions; others are forming them about you as well.

Your professional success has very little to do with your perception of others; rather, it has everything to do with the perception others have of you. The opinions people develop about you lead to the perceptions that become their reality—no matter what your intentions.

Of course, the perceptions others have of you may not, and often do not, match the way you feel about yourself. For example, a Citibank executive contacted me for executive coaching because others saw her as more self-assured than she actually was. She told me she often felt doubtful and insecure, and was surprised that her 360-degree review stated that she was viewed as the opposite—extremely confident and secure in herself. I told her, "Even though you are feeling something inside yourself that others don't notice, it's important to not let

> *Your professional success has very little to do with your perception of others; rather, it has everything to do with the perception others have of you.*

the feelings affect how you are viewed on the outside, especially when the view is positive."

You are constantly being judged, evaluated, and noticed at work and in your personal life. What you wear, what you say, how you interact, your attitude, and your behavior are all constantly being observed. When Arthur Collins joined the vice presidential ranks at Abbott Laboratories, the first thing he was told was that others would constantly be watching him: "You're going to be very surprised at how much people will watch what you do and listen to what you say. They'll take away much more than you think should be taken away from your words, little words or little things that you do."[2]

Once others observe, judge, and evaluate you, they're going to remember you exactly that way—whether you like it or not. That's why it's vital to give people an accurate picture of who you are or who you want to be to ensure that they see you in the exact way you prefer at work. If you don't, others will develop their own—frequently inaccurate—perceptions.

Your Behavior Affects Perception

Table 3.1 gives examples of the types of behavior you might be exhibiting, the positive perception you are trying to make, and the negative perception that may occur.

All of these examples prove that, despite your best intentions, you can be perceived in a variety of ways and you can never really tell what these might be. The only way to find out for sure is to ask, which we'll learn about in step 2.

TABLE 3.1 Perceptions of Types of Behavior You Might Be Exhibiting

Behavior	Positive Perception	Negative Perception
Laid-back and calm	In control	Lacks a sense of urgency
Keeping your office door closed	Focused on high-priority work	Not available, literally closed-off
Failing to complete work on time	Stickler for detail (taking the extra time to ensure that it's perfect)	Lazy and unreliable
Not speaking up at meetings	Agreeable team player	Doesn't care
Making quick decisions	Decisive	Makes snap decisions without thinking them through
Detail-oriented	Thorough	Unable to think strategically or look at the big picture
Asking for help	Not afraid to get help when needed	Can't work independently
Quiet and introspective	Thoughtful	Afraid to speak up
Doesn't readily share information	Respectful and protective of important information	Not a team player
Spends a lot time on phone and Internet	Strong multitasker	Not focused on what's important for the company
Frequently socializing	Networker	Not getting work done
Arrives late and leaves early	Efficient	Lacks commitment to the company
Treats all projects as equally important	Reliable, methodical	Unable to prioritize what is most important
Quick to say yes	Agreeable team player	Doesn't have a backbone; can't say no
Doing what is asked of you	Aims to please	Can't think outside the box and lacks initiative
Challenging everything	Demands excellence	Difficult to work with
Late for meetings	Busy, in high demand	Doesn't respect the people you work with
Has to be told to do something	Takes direction well	Lacks leadership skills
Wait for assignments to come to you	Nose to the grindstone	Lacks initiative
Shares knowledge, information, and expertise	Instructive, knowledgeable	Arrogant know-it-all
Complains about other employees	Expects the best from everyone	Not a team player
Doesn't take charge	Allows others to shine	Not a leader
Doesn't interact with others well	Private, independent	Has poor interpersonal skills
Avoids extra responsibilities	Has strong time management skills	Not a hard worker
Projects are quickly completed	Efficient and quick turnaround	Makes a lot of mistakes, rushes through tasks
Wants the most recognition when working on a team	Vocal, charismatic	Not a team player
Doesn't speak up, share, or initiate conversation	Pensive, prefers to observe	Not a good communicator and lacks confidence
Reluctant to inform others of your accomplishments	Modest	No one knows how great you are

Step 2: How You *Actually* Are Perceived

Do you know how you are perceived in your organization? You might think you do—but do you really? *Asking for feedback so you can learn what others think of you is one of the effective ways toward changing perception.*

A study conducted by one of the United States' foremost executive coaches, Marshall Goldsmith, reports that 95 percent of the leaders who ask for feedback are perceived more favorably than those whose don't. He continues, "By asking for feedback, analyzing the results, developing a focused action plan for change, and following up, leaders are perceived as more effective."[3]

A new Google employee reached out to me for executive coaching. She didn't know how her colleagues perceived her, and it was causing her to doubt her own abilities. She had just finished a major project and used this opportunity to ask the project manager to debrief with her so she could gain valuable feedback. During the meeting, she made it clear that she wanted honest feedback about how she had done and what she could learn for next time. She accomplished two things by initiating the feedback meeting. First, she got valuable feedback, which in this case was largely positive and helped build her confidence. This, in turn, influenced the project manager's perception of her. He now saw her as someone who wanted to improve both herself and the work she was doing for the company. Her commitment to high-quality work, continued self-reflection, development of key leadership skills, and good upward communication were critical factors in this project manager's decision to promote her eight months later.

Don't just wait for your next appraisal for feedback. Look for other opportunities to gauge how others perceive you. For example, you might ask a colleague after a contentious meeting, "How did I handle the problem with Paul?

Was I too defensive?" Be open to honest criticism and thank others for sharing their perceptions. Bill Amelio, former president and CEO of computer manufacturer Lenovo, has leveraged honest feedback to improve his perception and performance. "It's great if you have people in the organization who can tell you the truth no matter what. I have always been fortunate to work with people who were willing to give me feedback—even if they were not my direct manager. I have had people who would tell me if something was out of line or not quite right because they wanted me to be successful and knew that honest, direct feedback would help me execute and achieve."[4]

A client executive at Amazon.com told me he had a colleague who tended to suck all the oxygen out of the room during meetings. He said this person was brilliant, but he talked way too much and annoyed everyone around him. As a result, people tuned him out. He never knew this, because people weren't willing to tell him and he never asked for feedback on how he was perceived.

Many people are afraid to take this step. It can be daunting to know how you are being perceived. You may worry that you'll discover something you don't want to know. It can feel risky and vulnerable to ask how others perceive you. You may be concerned that you'll be perceived as insecure or without direction. As former Charles Schwab CEO David Pottruck remarked, "We all want to be stroked, admired, and complimented, but we have to be willing to listen to feedback we don't want to hear."[5]

California-based film studio Pixar is one of the most successful animation studios ever. With 26 Academy Awards and over $6.3 billion earned from its films, the company has a secret ingredient that has led to its success. Mark Murphy, CEO of *Leadership IQ*, explains, "At Pixar, when a director hits a snag on a film, they immediately call in the 'brain trust.' This is a group of brilliant senior filmmakers who come in, evaluate the film in progress, and give brutally honest feedback for about two hours. As President Ed Catmull says, 'It's far better to learn about problems when there's still time to fix them than from the audience after it's too late.'"[6]

Your career is similar to the filmmaking process at Pixar: It should always be something for which you make time to improve. It's never too late to do so. Ask for feedback by having a brain trust to provide honest and beneficial criticism and advice. Even if you are afraid, you must ask for input and pointers. People *do* have an opinion about you; it's wise to know what they are actually thinking. In a *Harvard Business Review* blog, author Sharon Daniels points out, "You might find it awkward to request feedback or painful to face unpleasant truths. There's no hiding from being judged, though, because a manager's shortcomings are on full view for everyone, even if the manager denies them."[7] It does take a lot of courage to ask others what they think of you. The responses you receive, however, will be more than worth it, since they'll reveal behaviors that others are judging and of which you might be unaware.

In the book *The Transparency Edge*, the authors state, "In leadership surveys of 559 managers, 86 percent of 6,023 of their followers and peers said that those leaders could improve at regularly asking for feedback."[8] You must be proactive and ask for feedback. Don't wait for it to come to you.

People in positions of power or authority don't always like giving feedback, because doing so can be stressful and difficult. They have to be honest, direct, and skillful in their delivery, and endure a confrontational process that takes courage. The same goes for your direct reports. They tend to not want to give feedback to someone in a professionally higher position. "The more senior and the more important you become, the less your subordinates will tell you the 'awful truth'—things that are difficult to hear, but that you need to

> There's no hiding from being judged.
> —Sharon Daniels

know," says Harvard Business School professor Robert S. Kaplan.[9]

In addition to requesting feedback informally, two formal structures can be applied. First, 360-degree feedback performance appraisals are helpful in providing insights about how others perceive you. Second, upward performance appraisals, during which managers ask their employees to share their opinions of them, are also constructive. Lenovo's Bill Amelio learned early in his career at automotive and engineering company AlliedSignal the importance of 360-degree feedback. "As I read the report, I was actually getting angry and marking [it] up. Then, I suddenly 'got it.' . . . I could either ignore the truth, or I could do something about it, change and become more effective. That was a major 'a-ha' moment for me . . . you have to be prepared and be willing to accept feedback."[10]

A client of mine at Microsoft was respected and talented, did her job extremely well, and had an impeccable reputation. I interviewed six people in preparation for her 360-degree feedback. Two individuals, the executive who was two levels above her and his peer, both stated that they wished she came to them more often to ask for advice and mentorship. Both of these top executives wanted more time with her due to her valuable opinions and thought processes. She was shocked to learn that these executives felt this way. This feedback prompted her to engage these executives more, and she became the team leader on one of their pet projects.

The business world isn't the only place where perceptions matter, of course. National Basketball Association (NBA) player Kobe Bryant has won five championships with the Los Angeles Lakers and has been an all-star 11 times. Yet even he reached the point in his career when he wasn't content with his level of success. Even though he had already established himself as one of the best in the world at his sport, he realized he could continue to grow and become better.

Bryant discovered that the teams the Lakers played had scouting reports, statistical theories, and analyses with complex notes on how to defend against Bryant and how best to limit him so that the other team could win the game. He realized that if he could gain this type of information, he could become even better.

Bryant didn't just want to be the best; he wanted to be the best *ever*. His determination for greatness gave him the impetus to seek out honest feedback. To that end, he hired basketball expert Mike Procopio, who began digging up everything he could on the ways opposing coaches and scouts believed Bryant could be vulnerable. Procopio said the following of Bryant: "One of the best winners ever in the history of the NBA, but he's seeking out help. He wants that edge and that's what makes him great. He could live without me, but he likes to have people around him who work hard and will tell him the truth.[11] Kobe wanted the honest and critical truth and was eager to learn as much as he could, like a child learning for the first time. After a win or a loss, he would say, 'Mike, what did you see that I can do better? What didn't I do? How are they going to guard me next time?'"[12]

Procopio shipped Bryant the reports for every regular-season game and throughout the NBA finals, which the Lakers won. Bryant said, "If these people think this stuff works, then I want to see what they're looking at and make my adjustments accordingly, if this is how they decide they want to play me."[13]

If one of the world's best athletes can look for ways to improve, then the rest of us certainly can as well. All of my clients consistently show a desire to become better, and I know that they aren't alone in this quest. By reading this book (and getting this far), you've proven that you're dedicated to improving yourself as well—to becoming the best you can be. Feedback will help you get there. Understanding what others think of you is vital for your improvement and growth.

Seek out feedback from others, especially from the ones who aren't afraid to tell you how they really feel. Dell Computer CEO Michael Dell isn't afraid of hearing the truth about what opinions others have of his company. He actively seeks feedback from customers. *Harvard Business Review on Leadership* explains, "Michael Dell himself also logs on to the Internet on a daily basis, scanning the bulletin boards and chat rooms used most frequently by industry insiders and computer devotees for information and opinions about market trends and for reactions to his company—and his competitors'—products."[14]

How to Ask for Feedback

The leader of the past was a person who knew how to tell. The leader of the future will be a person who knows how to ask.

—Peter Drucker
American writer, deemed the father of modern management

Choose two people from whom you can solicit honest feedback. You can ask for feedback from your boss, your boss's manager, your own direct reports, people who report to your direct reports, customers, peers, friends, and other colleagues. In other words, you can even ask someone who doesn't report to you or someone outside the organization. Before doing so, make sure to leverage these key strategies:

- **CHOOSE THE RIGHT TIME AND PLACE TO ASK.**

    Select a time and setting in which you and the other person aren't busy or preoccupied with other matters. Conduct the conversation in a private place where there will be minimal distractions. It's also a good idea to schedule the meeting in advance to allow that person the time to mull over an honest opinion of you, and not just offer off-the-cuff responses. Advance scheduling also emphasizes the fact that you're serious and you consider this a priority.

- **EXPLAIN WHY YOU'RE INTERESTED IN LEARNING HOW YOU'RE PERCEIVED.**

  Be sincere and honest. You might say, "I want to make sure I'm projecting a professional image, Sarah. You've seen me interact with customers and vendors when we've had problems. How do I come across in those situations?"

- **MAKE IT CLEAR YOU'RE NOT FISHING FOR COMPLIMENTS; YOU REALLY DO WANT AN HONEST ASSESSMENT.**

  People may hold back or tell you what they think you want to hear if they're afraid to hurt your feelings or they worry that you might become defensive. Sometimes it helps to admit a personal flaw or shortcoming to encourage people to open up. For example, "I know I can become impatient and sometimes interrupt people to state my point. I'm trying to work on that. Are there other behaviors people have mentioned to you about my personal style?"

- **ABOVE ALL—*DON'T* BE DEFENSIVE!**

  Even though you don't intend to, you may come across as defensive by the language you use. When someone shares less than positive feedback, avoid confrontational, in-your-face questions like "What do you mean?" or "Why do you say that?" or "Does everybody feel that way about me?"

- **ASK FOR SPECIFIC EXAMPLES.**

  If the feedback is critical or sensitive, take the emotion out of the situation by focusing on specific examples of the behavior in question. "Gosh, Jim, I didn't realize that some people think I always have to do it my way. I certainly don't want to give that impression. Can you think of any situations recently where I've done that, or where I might have turned some people off?"

- **THANK THEM FOR THEIR FEEDBACK.**

   Make it clear you appreciate their feedback, and show that you're serious about self-improvement by enlisting their help in the future. For example, "I'll try to focus on not dominating conversations, Judy. I really do want to hear other people's opinions. But if I suffer a relapse, let me know, okay? Just give me a friendly reminder, if you would. I promise I won't take it personally."

- **REPEAT THE PROCESS WITH OTHERS.**

   Solicit feedback from others to confirm or clarify areas that indicate a need for improvement or attention. Look for patterns or common themes.

- **DEVELOP AN ACTION PLAN TO ADDRESS THE NEGATIVE PERCEPTIONS.**

   If you handled these feedback sessions skillfully, you now have valuable intelligence that can go a long way toward making you an effective worker/boss/colleague. Develop an action plan to address the negative perceptions you may be creating, and look for opportunities to empha- size the positive perceptions you hope to convey.

- **REPORT BACK WITH AN UPDATE TO THE PERSON YOU APP- ROACHED FOR FEEDBACK.**

   After taking action and implementing the ideas shared in the "asking for feedback" conversation, follow up with the person who provided it. Give a detailed account of what you did, what you learned, and any positive behavior change that occurred. Let that person know how he or she has helped you in this process. Be appreciative.

The Feedback Conversation

There are countless people with whom you can have a feedback conversation: your immediate manager, a peer, another col- league to whom you don't report, someone senior to you, your boss's boss, a major customer/client, or people you interact with inside and outside the organization. Here are some questions you can ask:

- What do I do well?
- What could I do better?
- How am I perceived at this company?
- What are *your* perceptions of me, both negative and positive?
- How do I change the negative perceptions? What steps do I take to change them?
- What do you suggest I should be doing to improve others' perception of me?
- What can you do to help me create the right perception?

When you begin the conversation, make sure you explain the logic of why you are asking for feedback. This will help make the conversation a bit more normal, and make it seem less like you are needy or overly concerned about what others think. Explain the purpose of the feedback meeting in advance of it actually happening. This helps manage the other person's expectations so that he or she isn't shocked or surprised by the questions you ask. Some possible ways to introduce the discussion are:

- "I am doing a bit of self-evaluation and looking for some ways to grow my career. I talked to my boss already and felt it would be beneficial to speak to other people with whom I work. I want to know how you think I am performing and what your perception of me is. I value what you have to say."
- "I know you are someone with whom I work indirectly. I would like to learn about myself and the ways I can improve in this company. I respect you as a person and would therefore appreciate your feedback."

- "I want to improve my performance. I am asking for honest feedback because I know you are aware of and see things that would be helpful for me to know about."

Step 3: How You *Want* to Be Perceived

This third step focuses on creating the ideal perception you are seeking, the image you want to project. It allows you to take control of how others see you by being clear about how you want to be perceived.

- WHAT CHARACTER TRAITS MAKE THE RIGHT IMPRESSION?

    What qualities does a person with the right perception have at your company? For example, do such people convey confidence as business leaders? Are they respected as authorities? Do they create impact, exercise influence, provide value, know how to be noticed, stand out, create visibility, work on high-profile projects, continue to increase responsibility, and drive business results? Use specific terms to describe how you want to be perceived by others. Write down three adjectives that best describe how you want your colleagues to see you. Make those three words as powerful and expressive as possible. For example, don't settle for *smart* when *resourceful* suggests so much more, or use *committed* instead of *hard worker*. Once you create your short list, use it as a template for situations that require decisions or actions. Do your words and behavior lend credence to the perceptions you desire to create?

- ANTICIPATE YOUR NEXT CAREER PROGRESSION.

    Let's say that you want to move to one or two levels above where you are now. What kind of perception do you need others to have of you to be considered for this higher-level position? You could ask yourself, "How can I act more like [whatever position I want] in my current job?" Read the job description of the position to which you aspire in order to see the qualities and priorities associated with that position. This will help you develop a vision for the future that helps guide your professional development. Get to know the type of people who hold those positions. What qualities and characteristics do they exhibit? What are their backgrounds? How do they dress, talk, and behave? How do they conduct meetings, respond to questions, and interact with their managers, peers, and staff? Compare where you are to where you want to be. Decide what needs to change, and take action on it. In the meantime, do as William James suggested: "Act as if." Act as if you already have changed, and those changes will soon become a part of you.

For example, you might be a manager who wants to become a vice president. Wake up each day and say to yourself, "Today I am going to act as if I'm the VP of this company. I am not going to wait for my company to recognize that I am capable of doing the job." At first it might be quite a stretch and may move you out of your comfort zone. But soon enough, you'll start living what you expect to become your reality. Eliminate anything you are doing that limits your ability to act and think on that next level. Experiment with behaviors at your current level so that when you actually arrive at the next one, you will make fewer mistakes and will succeed effortlessly.

• **IDENTIFY THE PEOPLE YOU RESPECT.**

Think about all the people, dead or alive, that you respect. They can be famous people, individuals with whom you have worked, family members, friends, colleagues, or mentors. What is your perception of them? What about them do you respect? What have they done to positively affect the way you think about them? You will notice characteristics you desire in yourself as you answer these questions. As you compile this list, you can identify which traits you want for your ideal state of perception.

Step 4: How You *Change* Perception

> *Perception can be changed in a short amount of time.*

It is difficult to change someone's negative perception of you. It only takes one mistake, bad move, or missed deadline to begin eroding the positive reputation you've developed. Negative opinions are so difficult to change because the way someone sees you becomes their reality, even though what they think may not be true. Even if the majority of the people who work with you have positive perceptions of you, you still want to focus on enhancing and improving perception continuously. This will help create the perception that you want reinforced.

It's important to remember that perception can be changed in a short amount of time. You don't have to fear that you have cemented a negative perception and feel hopeless about being able to change it. You *can* do something about it right now. The following are real-life examples of goals that my clients have accomplished in less than a week, after which they immediately began to change the perception others had of them:

- You typically haven't been participating in conversations, but you suddenly start speaking up at meetings.
- You are usually someone who enters a room and dominates and takes over. However, you instead begin standing back, and sharing only when you have something important and pressing to contribute.
- You begin sharing your accomplishments and impact on the firm instead of just letting your work speak for itself.

One of the important steps toward changing perception is to become aware of the unspoken reward system inside your organization. This system

> *An influential individual sharing how great you are has a lot more impact than you can achieve on your own.*

isn't about pay or bonuses; it's about the subtle recognition given out by decision makers on a daily basis. For example, why did Jill gain that plum assignment? Why was George asked to head up a prestigious committee when the regular chair was on vacation? Why was Carlos asked to brief a group of executives from another division about your work group's latest breakthrough? Instead of being jealous or resentful, assess these situations as objectively as possible, and consider the perceptions that company leaders have of these individuals. Now consider the perceptions they might have of you for each situation. Where do you fall short? What tangible steps can you take to positively influence those perceptions?

The following are 10 specific steps you can take to reinforce a positive perception and/or to change a negative one.

Ten Ways to Enhance, Improve, and Change Perception

1. **IDENTIFY ADVOCATES WHO CAN SPEAK ON YOUR BEHALF.**

    Take advantage of having someone else act as an advocate for you. This is someone who will campaign on your behalf, champion your cause, and help improve others' perception of you. They will speak up about your accomplishments to others, which can be extremely beneficial to someone who is not comfortable tooting one's own horn. With a strong advocate working on your behalf, you don't have to aggressively self-promote. An influential individual sharing how great you are has a lot more impact than you can achieve on your own. See Chapter 5 for details on how to make the most from your advocate relationship.

2. **BE ASSIGNED TO HIGHLY VISIBLE PROJECTS AT WORK.**

When you work on projects that have high visibility, you have the opportunity to directly affect how others perceive you. This influence can help you enhance others' respect for you.

One way to get started is to identify a project that your boss's boss deems most important. Discuss this project with your immediate boss, and create a plan on how you can do more work for it. When you add value to this highly visible project, your boss's manager's perception of you will become increasingly approving.

3. **HAVE YOUR MANAGER (AND EVEN HIS OR HER BOSS) ACKNOWLEDGE YOUR CONTRIBUTIONS PUBLICLY.**

It helps to have someone else speaking up on your behalf when you're trying to improve others' perception of you. Ask if they would share praise, discuss your successes, and emphasize the impact you've had on the company. Others will start to see the value you provide to the company when your superiors consistently extol your achievements publicly.

Choose a specific project, idea, or situation that provided value to your group or company, and let your boss know about all the hard work, leadership, and value you contributed to it.

The more details you can provide, the better. For example, a client of mine shared a recent success with her boss by letting him know that she had suggested an idea for a new product and helped launch it to seven new field offices, which added over $13 million in sales. Now the boss could publicly discuss her accomplishment with others.

When your manager understands the complete impact you've had on the bottom line, he or she will be inclined to acknowledge you openly. You might have to ask your boss to share this information. You can do this by describing how getting credit and recognition publicly would benefit both of you and the organization as whole: It would help your career, make your boss look good, and create a positive outlook for the team.

4. **ENCOURAGE YOUR BOSS TO SHARE WITH HIS OR HER BOSS YOUR OVERALL VALUE TO THE FIRM.**

Making your boss's manager aware of how well you are doing enhances this positive perception of you. The more your superiors appreciate what an important commodity you are to the organization, the more they'll value you. Having managers exalt their employees' wins to higher-ups has an especially powerful impact because so few managers actually do this.

Express your desire to have your boss share your value, wins, and contributions to his or her own boss. Explain to your immediate manager how your success reflects positively on him or her. The increased exposure to your boss's boss will likely bring you more responsibility, and that will free up your immediate boss to do more important projects, making it a win-win situation for everyone involved.

5. **EDUCATE MANAGEMENT ABOUT WHAT YOU DO AND WHAT YOUR POSITION IS IN THE COMPANY.**

Management has a tendency to see you as a replaceable commodity, and often takes what you do for granted. Educate your managers about how valuable your position is and let them know about everything you do to make your job work as well as it does. As you provide them with a more accurate picture of all you do, they will begin to alter how they view your position.

Choose two people in upper management who need to better understand the importance of what you do and your position in the company. Find a reason to engage them in conversation at least once a week by seeking them out at meetings or sending them an e-mail. Prepare yourself for each communication by identifying the specific actions you've taken and tasks you've completed that provide them with a comprehensive picture of your position's significance.

6. **GAIN EXPOSURE TO INFLUENTIAL CORPORATE LEADERS.**

When you can interact with your organization's senior leaders, you can directly change and improve perception. Ask your boss for opportunities that will allow you increased exposure to these types of leaders. If discussing it with your boss is not an option, aggressively seek out projects that will provide you the necessary interaction with these leaders. Attend meetings and sit next to these senior people. Engage them in conversation, ask impressive questions, or share the successes you've achieved on projects.

7. **KNOW THE IMPACT YOU HAVE ON OTHERS.**

As you take the time to notice your effect on others, you will begin to see what kind of impact you actually are having on them. Most of the time you aren't aware at all of how what you are doing actually influences others. Your increased awareness will help you notice the consequences of your actions, and the effects they have on others' perception of you. This is where perception can be positively altered.

Start to take notice of how your work impacts others. Take notes after each interaction by proactively looking for and identifying the effect you have. Additionally, ask people how your work is benefiting them; their answers will help you see more clearly exactly what value you provide.

8. **SURROUND YOURSELF WITH PEOPLE WHOM OTHERS RESPECT.**

As we've already determined, the group you hang out with at work reflects back on you—so be selective about the people with whom you align yourself. Make sure you interact with people who have influence, are respected, and are solid leaders whom people admire. Be careful not to engage with people who gossip, undermine others, aren't team players, or care only about themselves.

How can you determine who fits into these categories? Observe people at work, and figure out which ones have the best reputations and where respect and credibility are evident. Find ways to interact with at least one or two influential people. Learn about their interests so you can find common ground in discussions. If they participate on any work committees or non-work-related volunteer activities, become involved in the same ones.

9. **TAKE THE LEAD ON A PROJECT.**

If you are working on a project as a team member, see if you can become the team lead. This is the person who represents the group and discusses their progress when the manager wants to know how the project is going. This will provide high visibility and will influence how people perceive you, since the team lead is often the one who presents information to members of management. Management will see you as someone who can take charge, even though the entire team worked on the project together.

Discuss your desire to be the team lead on a project with your boss, and find out what you need to do to make this happen. Implement these suggestions so that you can make your case and prove your worth as a team lead. Reach out and seek support from peers, mentors, and prior team leads on the gaps you need to fill to successfully procure this kind of position.

10. **STOP PERPETUATING ALL NEGATIVE PERCEPTIONS.**

Make a list of how top management and your peers currently perceive you. If there are negative perceptions, write down how you would like to be viewed instead. Then carefully monitor your behavior at work to make sure you are reinforcing the positive traits while deemphasizing the negative ones.

Summary and Action Steps

In the next section, we'll be focusing on the importance of visibility. Before we do, here are the Chapter 3 summary and action steps.

Summary

Create the right perception. The perception management process involves four steps:

- *Step 1: How you* think *you are perceived.* This step provides surprising evidence that how you *think* you are perceived does not always match how you *actually* are perceived. In Table 3.1 you saw a list of over two dozen different examples of the various ways in which others might see you versus how you see yourself.

- *Step 2: How you* actually *are perceived.* You can discover a lot about perception by asking for feedback. This can be a difficult task to accomplish because both the asker and giver of feedback may feel vulnerable in the process. There are many strategies and conversation-starting questions to help you ask for and gather feedback more easily and comfortably.

- *Step 3: How you* want *to be perceived.* This step will help you create your desired reputation. Be clear on how you want others to view you. Identify the character traits of the people you respect, and determine which ones you want to emulate. Discern the desired perception you need others to have of you for you to achieve the next step in your career.

- *Step 4: How you* change *perception.* A single mistake can ruin your reputation. The perception others have of you *can* be changed. Implement each of the 10 suggestions to improve your perception.

Take Action Now

- How do you *think* you're perceived at work? Observe your behavior for the next two weeks and record how you *think* you are perceived.

- Observe your interactions with people in both work and life. Take notice of what your internal opinions and judgments of them are.

- Review Table 3.1 types of behaviors that impact perception, and put a checkmark next to the behaviors that you exhibit. Do these behaviors create the desired perception? If not, come up with ways that you can transform this perception into something more beneficial.

- Review all nine points in the "How to Ask for Feedback" section. Next, review "The Feedback Conversation" and the seven questions to ask. Then, select three people to ask for feedback on how you are perceived in the organization. They could be your boss, your boss's boss, your direct reports, people who report to your direct reports, customers, peers, friends, or colleagues.

- Ask yourself about the level above your position: "How can I act more like I'm already at *that level* in my current job?" Identify the characteristics and behaviors of someone at this level whom you respect. Choose three of these behaviors to adopt in your current job.

- Identify two people you respect, and figure out why you feel this way. What do (or did) they do to create this level of respect? Once you answer these two questions, look over your answers and select the characteristics you want to develop in yourself.

- How do you *want* to be perceived by others? Write down what this ideal state specifically looks like. Then take your ideal state and compare it to how you actually are perceived. Notice the discrepancy between these two states, and identify three ways you can create your ideal perception.

• Review the "Ten Ways to Enhance, Improve, and Change Perception," and apply all 10 suggestions to your work. Choose one per week to implement over the next 10 weeks.

Part One—Perception Conclusion

Bonus Online Material

How are you perceived at work? Do you influence how others see you? Take the free assessment at www.Garfinkle ExecutiveCoaching.com/assessments-perception.html to find out. Through this evaluation, you'll learn the top 10 areas you must emphasize to improve your image among those who matter most.

You've learned the importance of perception management. You know how to influence how others see you, and you have the ability to create the right perception that reflects who you truly are. Your value to and impact on the organization will be clearly known. The success of your career is in your hands. With perception firmly established and understood, let's move to the importance of visibility.

Part Two

Increase Your Visibility—Stand Out
and Get Noticed by the People
Who Matter Most

4

Up Your Visibility

There is only one thing in life worse than being talked about, and that is not being talked about.

—Oscar Wilde
Irish poet and writer

Be Memorable

Every four years, Olympic athletes compete and achieve incredible feats that make us remember them. Whether it's Michael Phelps's record-setting eight gold medals, 14-year-old Nadia Comaneci's seven perfect-10 scores, Mary Lou Retton becoming the first American to win the gymnastics all-around, or 1980's "Miracle on Ice" U.S. hockey team, these moments are etched in our brains. How can these points of time be so memorable when the Olympics last just a little over two weeks?

These events stay top of the mind because of their impact. The impression they have on us makes them unforgettable. These athletic moments stand out above the rest of the 400 events in which the other 13,000 athletes compete because something remarkable happens that is cemented in our memories.

How can you as an individual stand out just like these incredible Olympians? You must identify specific achievements you've made and are making that are remarkable, are distinctive in their results, and truly make a difference to the company. Discern which of your behaviors cause you to stand out from the crowd, and what actions captivate others and capture their attention. In short, what do you do that makes a difference? What do you bring to certain situations that others don't?

Kathy Hollenhorst, the former senior vice president of marketing at Caribou Coffee, understood that Caribou had to do something unique to stand out from its giant competitor Starbucks. So she asked, "What does Caribou have that Starbucks doesn't?" This type of questioning prompted Caribou to create licensing deals with unusual partners such as General Mills and Kemp's Ice Cream. By distinguishing itself from the competition, Caribou became the second-largest coffee chain in the United States.[1]

Ask yourself the same question: "What do I have that my successful colleagues don't have?" Visibility does not just mean that you have to be physically visible. It also means that your work has to be so unique and outside-of-the-box that it becomes your signature.

Highlight what you do that is memorable. Showcase your talents, skills, results, value, and overall impact. Produce excellent work and be remarkable so that you become noticed. It's a shame to work hard, be intelligent, and strive for excellence and still not become a known commodity. People, especially those beyond your direct group, must become aware of you. You must make an impression on others to have impact and be remembered. As Seth Godin explains in his book *Purple Cow*, "Something remarkable is worth talking about. Worth noticing. Exceptional. New. Interesting. It's a Purple Cow. Boring stuff is invisible. It's a brown cow."[2]

If You Are Not Visible, You Are Invisible

The hard fact is that limited exposure means limited visibility, which means limited advancement opportunities.

—Curtis J. Crawford
American computer systems engineer and director of DuPont

Name a leader who *isn't* visible. Chances are that you can't. To be a leader you must be visible. Leadership and visibility require each other. When you have both, people will see you as someone with power, influence, authority, and leadership. They'll know who you are and what you do, and will appreciate the value you provide. Without visibility, you won't be noticed, and your career progression will come to an abrasive halt.

The importance of visibility may not seem obvious. Perhaps working hard and producing results have been enough during your early career experiences for others to take notice and compensate the good work you've done. You may have received past promotions based solely on merit and hard work. Your career may for a time move ahead nicely until suddenly—*bam*—it comes to a standstill.

This can occur when you come to a point in your career where you are successful, but stuck. Talent and ability to perform take you only so far. Be warned: *If you don't proactively leverage and utilize visibility, your career will stagnate.* A client of mine confessed to me, "I've reached a plateau where my talents and skills aren't enough. I used to feel that I had my success under *my* control, and I don't anymore. My growth plan was once clear; I knew exactly what I needed to do to gain my next promotion. Now that I've jumped to the management level, the path is not as obvious. It's not a documented process anymore. I need to initiate a visibility plan so I am noticed, or my career will stall."

> *Without visibility, you won't be noticed, and your career progression will come to an abrasive halt.*

What happened? No one alerted you that you were going to hit a professional wall that would demand that you learn and apply a new trait for success—increased visibility. *Visibility is important because the people who make decisions about your career need to be aware of your value.* You might be performing well, but unless the right people know how well you are performing, you'll be overlooked, especially if you work in a group of very talented people. The key is to actively inform others of your value so that you reach the most influential individuals' radar screens. Dorie Clark in the *Harvard Business Review* blog advises, "No matter how brilliant and talented you are, you won't be sufficiently appreciated within your organization or by your customers until the broader public recognizes you."[3]

Get Noticed by the People Who Matter Most

Visibility refers literally to making your good works and yourself visible (or seen by) influential people.

—Andrew J. DuBrin
Professor of Management at the College of Business,
Rochester Institute of Technology

Keith Ferrazzi, author of the best-selling book *Never Eat Alone* (Crown Business, 2005), graduated from Harvard Business School with a tough choice: to join either Deloitte or McKinsey Consulting. Former head of Deloitte Consulting Pat Loconto recalls that before accepting the offer, Ferrazzi insisted on seeing the organization's "head guys." According to Loconto, Ferazzi also stated at this meeting that "he would accept the offer on one condition . . . he and I would have dinner once a year . . . so I promised to have dinner with him once a year, and that's how we recruited him . . . that way, he was guaranteed access to the top."[4]

Ferrazzi went on to become the youngest partner in Deloitte Consulting's history.

> *You cannot solely rely on putting your head down, doing your work well, and going home.*
> —Monica Mandelli

Increasing visibility means presenting yourself in a way that compels people to take notice. You must be impressive, show others your talents and skills, and have them acknowledge what you offer the organization. When others know about you, they are able to recognize your value, appreciate your contribution to the company, and leverage your talents.

Of course, it can be difficult for some people to make others aware of the work they've done. For over 30 years, pioneering researchers George W. Dudley and Shannon L. Goodson have studied the reasons behind people's fear of self-promotion. One five-year analysis focused on the salary increases and promotions that managers received, and provided this conclusion: "We found those who were promoted most often and given the biggest salary increases did not necessarily turn out to be those judged to be the most technically competent. *It was those who were most willing to make whatever level of competence they had visible.*"[5]

Managing director of the investment management division at Goldman Sachs Monica Mandelli says this about the importance of visibility: "It took me a while to figure out that you cannot solely rely on putting your head down, doing your work well, and going home. You need to step up and courageously market yourself. You need to make sure people are fully aware of what you are contributing." She added, "You need to make sure that people know who you are."[6]

The Benefits of Increasing Visibility

All leaders need to be visible to be seen and to be seen to be effective.
—Ian Jackman
American author

Choosing to prioritize and constantly focus on increasing your visibility grants you three major benefits: enhanced confidence, willingness to take risks and be known, and elimination of fear of failure. First, with increased visibility comes enhanced confidence. As you put yourself out there in high-profile situations and succeed, you increase your own belief in yourself.

Second, growing visibility is accompanied by a willingness to take risks—and every chance that you take presents you with new opportunities to become known and operate outside of your comfort zone. Author Umesh Ramakrishnan reinforces this point in his book *There's No Elevator to the Top* when he says, "At the very least, volunteering for the difficult jobs and being prepared to take risks will get you noticed." Risk taking is one action that can significantly differentiate you from your peers, since it shows that you are willing to do something that others aren't willing to do.

Third, visibility helps to eliminate fear of failure. Just imagine everything you would do if you weren't afraid of not doing it successfully. Would you take on that project that everyone else is scared to accept? Would you assume responsibility that is beyond your comfort zone? Would you choose to put your name in the running for that management position? Would you directly express your thoughts and ideas to members of upper management? All three of these areas—confidence, risk taking, and elimination of fear of failure—directly affect you and your mind-set.

Build Confidence

The fascinating thing about visibility is that you generate an increasing amount of confidence as you become *more* visible. Your self-assurance continues to build like a wave in the ocean. As you undertake more opportunities to be visible, you will build a deep reservoir of confidence. This sureness you have in yourself then serves as the impetus to prompt you to be visible over and over again—no matter what the repercussions might be. You are secure in who you are and what you are capable of; you believe in your abilities and have a solid sense of self. Because of this trust in yourself, you want to put yourself out there and be a bit fearless in making yourself and your talents known.

Confidence is a necessary characteristic to develop as you climb the corporate ladder—and the higher the stakes, the greater the responsibility. As you take on challenging projects, your confidence becomes even more of a necessity. You want a greater sense of self-assurance than you have today, and the only way to help propel you toward that level is to seek out situations to immediately become visible and prove to yourself that you are more capable than maybe even *you* had imagined.

Take Risks

Visibility and risk taking go together; one cannot exist without the other, since becoming visible requires you to step out of your comfort zone and take chances. As one of Goldman Sachs's managing directors, Melissa Goldman, says, "When it comes to your success and differentiating yourself, taking risks is a critical part. You have to take some risk to get the reward."[7] Even though you take somewhat of a chance with each opportunity to increase your visibility, you also gain countless benefits. You are exposed to influential executives; you show others your talents and skills; your value becomes known; and others recognize how to leverage you for their benefit.

As you become comfortable taking risks, you enjoy a greater sense of freedom to continue to do so with diminished concern for any downsides. You've experienced over and over again the benefits gained by taking risks, so you become more comfortable engaging in this kind of behavior. These advantages help you establish a mind-set that focuses less and less on what others think or what judgments they make. You will have the confidence to take risks and gain the necessary visibility for your advancement.

There will be situations in which the risk you take results in negative judgment. This is often what causes people to feel reluctant to make themselves visible. Once you stop taking risks, you do less, and therefore become less visible. There might even appear to be some benefits to this lack of visibility; you may feel safe since you no longer are making a poor impression to someone important inside the company. However, you'll arrive at a point in your career where everyone around you will be just as good as or even better than you. You'll realize that you can't just cruise along without increasing your visibility. As one of my clients told me, "If you are coasting and not pedaling, you can only be going downhill." You must be constantly visible so others know you, see your value, demand you more, seek you out, and require you to be a member of their team. Taking risks is a necessity at this stage of your career.

Do Not Fear Failure

Most people have some level of fear when it comes to making themselves visible. They worry that it's too risky to put themselves out there and become noticed. They are unaware of the positive effects of negative visibility and choose instead to hide out and avoid attracting attention.

Negative visibility comes from making a grave error, a costly mistake, or an incorrect statement at the wrong time. This isn't always irreversibly detrimental, though. Such slipups will prompt someone to keep an eagle eye on your performance and behavior—something that you can use to your advantage. You can take this extra attention on what you did wrong and diligently commit to make good on

> *You'll arrive at a point in your career where everyone around you will be just as good as or even better than you. You'll realize that you can't just cruise along without increasing your visibility.*

your errors. This is a great opportunity to change people's perception dramatically. The dedicated effort and actual changes in behavior will create the results that both you and others want. The fear of failure becomes minimized when you see the positive benefits of negative visibility.

You could be achieving great things and having a huge impact on the company, but it doesn't matter if no one knows about it. Making yourself known requires that you overcome this fear of failure. You can't hide out. People of influence must know you.

Research has shown that one thing human beings fear most—even more than death, in some cases—is public speaking. About three-quarters of the population have anxiety when it comes to addressing others in a public forum. What are they so afraid of? They fear being visible! When you speak in front of a group, you make yourself completely visible to your audience. You can't hide; you *have* to show up.

The key to eliminating the fear of failure is being willing to fail. According to Brad Bird, the Oscar-winning director of two animated feature films, success comes only when we open ourselves up to *not* playing it safe, to taking risks, and to being willing to fail: "The first step in achieving the impossible is believing that the impossible can be achieved. There was a point during the making of *The Incredibles* where we had a company meeting. We have them about twice a year, and anybody can bring up concerns. Somebody raised their hand and said, 'Is *The Incredibles* too ambitious?' [My colleague] Ed Catmull said, 'I don't know' and looked at me. I just said, 'No! If there's one studio that needs to be doing stuff that is "too ambitious," it's this one. You guys have had nothing but success. What do you do with it? You don't play it safe—you do something that scares you that's at the edge of your

> *You could be achieving great things and having a huge impact on the company, but it doesn't matter if no one knows about it.*

capabilities, where you might fail. That's what gets you up in the morning.'"[8]

The Progression of Visibility

Make visible what, without you, might have never been seen.
—Robert Bresson
French film director

So how does the process of becoming visible actually occur? How does someone go from just barely being noticed inside an organization to actually being valued and having impact? The first step in creating visibility is to be *noticed*—to have others in the organization become aware of you and your work. For people who are comfortable hiding out and not having others aware of them, it can be difficult to be seen at work. Getting noticed, however, is the initial necessary step toward becoming visible in the organization.

After becoming noticed, the next step is to actually *stand out*, which takes the courage and willingness to be exposed. It's not easy to put yourself out there for others to form an opinion, judge, and even possibly reject you. It involves raising your profile, becoming known inside the organization, and being outspoken. It requires that you inform others of your accomplishments, and be direct and candid in your decisions and opinions.

After you have begun to stand out, others will *recognize* you for what you are doing that is benefiting the organization. The recognition you receive is a vital source of positive feedback and is necessary at this stage in the visibility process. You'll begin to feel a bit uneasy with the amount of visibility you've generated as you work on making yourself known, and this uncomfortable edge brings a level of vulnerability. Therefore, the energy and enthusiasm from others' recognition provides you with the acknowledgment needed to conquer this feeling of uncertainty and keep moving forward.

Next in the visibility process is being *remembered*. People in the organization, especially ones who have influence, will begin to remember who you are. This takes place when you have established yourself as someone your colleagues know, see, appreciate, and respect. Every person wants to reach this stage—to be someone whom others turn to for knowledge and expertise.

After being remembered, you feel *valued*. You've become a known and desired commodity at your company. The people with whom you work know how much significance and importance you bring to the organization and therefore seek you out.

Once you have become valued, the final step in the visibility process is to make an *impact*. You've moved from being noticed and standing out to having a genuine, tangible effect on your company. You've become a valuable person whose efforts and input are necessary for the organization's current and future success (see Figure 4.1).

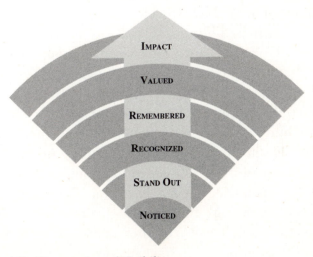

FIGURE 4.1 The Progression of Visibility

Two Types of Employees

There are two types of employees at any company: worker bees and roosters. Each one of these has a relationship to visibility that undermines one's career. By reading the descriptions that follow, you'll be able to see which one you are. You can also see if you recognize which of these describes your colleagues, direct reports, and senior management.

Worker Bees

Worker bees produce results, yet rarely are visible. Instead of trying to get others to notice their efforts, they simply focus on doing their jobs well. They contribute as much as they can at a result level and primarily care about performing their tasks as well as they can. Performance is what matters to them; they operate under the mind-set that "If I perform well, success will come." They believe that the work they do will speak for itself and that continuing to produce accomplishments will be enough to further their own advancement.

Client example: A client of mine who worked at Motorola came to me because she was quiet and didn't speak up at meetings. She sat in her cubicle working away. She produced excellent work, was incredibly smart, and was extremely competent at her job. However, not many people knew how valuable she was, because she wasn't good at making herself visible. She had a lot to say, but did so only via e-mail. She thought that she could simply let her work speak for itself, but this lack of visibility made it so that senior management didn't see how valuable she was to the organization. As her manager explained to me during 360-degee interviews, "I am afraid to give her any visibility. If I put her on a big project, she may not be assertive enough to drive the project. She hasn't given me confidence that I can trust her ability to own, lead, and take over the project."

Roosters

Roosters spend their time tooting their own horns and making themselves visible, but often for no good reason. They incessantly strut and crow about themselves. They keep talking, yet have done very little of substance to back up their claims of greatness. Roosters spend more time creating visibility than working on performance. They know how to stand out, look good, and have others notice them. They leverage their organization's inner politics to their advantage so they are seen in a positive light.

Once others look closely, however, they find that the work roosters are accomplishing doesn't warrant the amount of attention they demand or think they deserve. Once this disparity comes to light, the roosters are exposed for who they truly are and what they are actually doing to benefit the company, which isn't very much. In fact, when companies downsize, roosters are often the first to go.

Client example: A client who worked at Morgan Stanley received three promotions in two years. He exaggerated his results and got people to notice him, which worked for a while, as he received the promotions he wanted. However, he irritated many people as he advanced in the company. He would offend others by taking all of the credit for doing work when other people had made significant contributions. He constantly one-upped people by making his accomplishments seem better than anything anyone else had achieved. This became increasingly infuriating to his colleagues, especially because it came from such a self-absorbed place. His inability to back up his own claims of personal greatness ultimately led to his dismissal.

Even though you might relate to or know people who are worker bees or roosters, neither of these is a favorable persona. Rather, the ideal type of employee does valued work and showcases it appropriately. This person is the one who advances quickly because he or she has substance to back up self-promotion.

Such people understand the importance of both producing excellent work and exhibiting it to others. They show no hesitancy in sharing its value. Due to these individuals' naturally high degree of visibility, the talents and skills that help create their accomplishments are commonly known by people of influence within the company.

Client example: One client of mine, an executive at Visa International, enjoyed an extreme amount of success in a very short period of time. She became influential without having any positional authority. She produced excellent work, was a high performer, and made sure people knew how valuable she was. She wanted to utilize all her skills at work and be challenged to grow. She demonstrated her talents through the projects she managed, the people she led, and the senior executives with whom she collaborated. Once people learned of her accomplishments, she became valued for what she produced, and felt comfortable sharing it with others. The respect she had earned from her colleagues provided a level of credibility; because she was so authentic, no one questioned her motives.

So, which one of these are you? You might be the worker bee who is so focused on results that you spend little time making them visible. You might be the rooster who spends every moment seizing the promotional opportunity and therefore little time on your actual performance. The objective, of course, is for you to become an unstoppable employee who can support your visibility with the solidity of your performance.

Mind-Sets That Stunt Your Growth

There is only one cause of unhappiness: the false beliefs you have in your head, beliefs so widespread, so commonly held, that it never occurs to you to question them.

—Anthony de Mello
Priest and author

When clients hire me to work specifically on increasing visibility, often I have to dispel the crippling beliefs that are holding them back. It is frequently the way people think about themselves that limits their visibility and stunts their professional growth.

Each of the following limiting beliefs is connected to a corresponding consequence. Your career success is dependent on reversing these restrictive beliefs. Do you silently believe any of the following statements?

- I can't get ahead because nobody knows who I am or what I do for this company.
- Only my boss needs to know what I am doing.
- I've been involved in a lot of key projects, but my visibility in the organization is not high enough to receive major recognition.
- I lack opportunities for positive exposure and visibility.

Out of Sight, Out of Mind

- I CAN'T GET AHEAD BECAUSE NOBODY KNOWS WHO I AM OR WHAT I DO FOR THIS COMPANY.

  If you aren't visible, you won't be known. When people don't see you enough, they forget about you; it's as simple as that. Let's say that you receive a phone call from someone you haven't heard from in a few months. You begin to think about her in that moment, and perhaps for the rest of the day. When time passes and you don't talk with her again, you forget about her. This is why we make to-do lists of what needs to be done around the house and at work. We need reminders to keep these tasks at the forefront of our minds.

  You can't afford to be out of sight or out of mind in the workplace. Visibility is necessary to progress in your career. You have to make sure that others are constantly aware of your performance at work, and this requires repetition. Repetition doesn't mean repeatedly showcasing 5 or 10 times the one task you accomplished last week; rather, it means discussing one time each the 5 or 10 great tasks you accomplished. You must repeatedly advertise all that you have done that presents you in a positive light.

Advertising campaigns epitomize the positive effects of repetition. Anytime you buy something that has been advertised (which is essentially anything), you are witnessing the power of visibility. Paula Keaveney, author of *Marketing for the Voluntary Sector*, observes, "To absorb any message properly, we need to hear it, or see it, a number of times. The parallel of exam revision is useful here. Anyone who has learned a subject, and revised it for a test, knows that it takes a number of reviews before enough has been 'taken in.' Advertisers want their viewers, or readers, to take in a message well enough to prompt action. This is why repetition is vital."[9]

The purpose of an advertisement is to show you why you need that specific item. The benefits are clearly defined. Therefore, just as an advertisement does, you are showing everyone at work why they need you and what benefits you provide. By constantly showcasing your successes and talents, you make your value widely known.

My Work Will Speak for Itself

- **ONLY MY BOSS NEEDS TO KNOW WHAT I AM DOING.**
  "Research shows that doing great work won't guarantee you a promotion or a raise, and it may not even be

that important for keeping your job. What matters even more is your ability to get noticed, to influence the metrics used to measure performance, to figure out what matters to your boss . . . "[10]

Clients often ask me, "Why should I increase my visibility? Why can't I let my work speak for itself?" You may think that your skills will naturally make your worth known and that you don't need to do anything to be visible. Unfortunately, you are relying on luck, chance, and hope—three things that you should never

> *Research shows that doing great work won't guarantee you a promotion or a raise, and it may not even be that important for keeping your job. What matters even more is your ability to get noticed.*
> —Jeffrey Pfeffer

count on. My response has always been: "You can't assume decision makers are aware of your accomplishments or know the impact of your work and your value to the organization."

Many employees are passed by or completely overlooked simply because senior management doesn't know how valuable they are. In a *Newsweek* article, Deloitte & Touche USA's chairman of the board, Sharon Allen, is quoted as saying: "Take responsibility for your own career. Don't assume that others are aware of the good work you're doing. When I was a young accountant, I was unhappy about not getting a promotion. I went to my supervisor and told him all of these things that I thought I should be given credit for and he said, 'Well, gee, I didn't know that you had done all of these things.' It was a real wake-up call. You don't have to be a bragger, but I think it's very important that we make people aware of our accomplishments."[11]

> *Many employees are passed by or completely overlooked simply because senior management doesn't know how valuable they are.*

It's Not Just Who You Know That Counts; It's Who Knows You

- I'VE BEEN INVOLVED IN A LOT OF KEY PROJECTS, BUT MY VISI-
BILITY IN THE ORGANIZATION IS NOT HIGH ENOUGH TO RE-
CEIVE MAJOR RECOGNITION.

    You might know a lot of people, but the people with the power and influence have to be aware of your value and presence. Visibility is about making sure that others—particularly people of influence and importance—know your work. If your company has a meeting in which there are 10 people deciding whether you should be promoted, what will they say? Does everyone know you, your key accomplishments, and the value you bring to the company? If not, you are less likely to receive the promotion.

    Cisco Systems, Inc., operates under a system that underlines this importance. They make sure employees expand their network and interact with the influential executives. Economist Sylvia Ann Hewlett says that Cisco's Inclusive Advocacy Program "pairs the company's highest potential diverse talent—both men and women—with a VP or SVP 'advocate' in a different function and different geography over a nine-month period to expand the advocates' network of new sources of knowledge capital and the talents' network of influential contacts."[12]

    Cisco understands the importance of having other executives outside of an employee's immediate group of colleagues know this employee and his or her work. You can take a cue from this method and expand your network beyond your own direct coworkers. Get to know other executives, peers, and staff members outside of your business unit. This will help you in your career, because they will serve as advocates, mentors, resources, and support.

An executive client of mine at Marriott Hotels expressed the following viewpoint: "While I am visible up and down in my specific group—to my boss and his other directs and the people who report to me—I am not visible broadly . . . to my boss's peers, my boss's boss, and his boss. I was supposed to be made director and I wasn't. There were people outside my group who got promoted and I wasn't. This was a catalyst in my realizing that I had not sold my value broadly."

If You Don't Gain Credit for What You Have Done, Someone Else Will

- I LACK OPPORTUNITIES FOR POSITIVE EXPOSURE AND VISIBILITY.

  Make sure people know what you do and accomplish, so that you gain the appropriate credit. Receiving recognition for the work you have done requires that you ensure that others are aware of what you are doing. The more details they receive about your accomplishments and results, the less chance there is that someone else can take credit for your efforts. If you hide yourself, you make it easier for others to stand out. Even when you do the majority of work, the person who talks the loudest and takes a dominant stand is often the one who becomes associated with the bottom-line results.

Speak Up on Behalf of Your Work

A really great talent finds its happiness in execution.
—Johann Wolfgang von Goethe
German writer, author of *Faust*

Former local San Francisco TV host Ross McGowan was negotiating a contract with his boss. He was surprised when his boss made a fairly low offer, especially considering how high his programs' ratings were. McGowan asked why the offer was so low and his boss said, "You make it look so easy."

McGowan's boss's level of appreciation for him would have risen substantially if the boss saw a less skilled TV interviewer doing the same job with less ease. But just because McGowan made his job look easy and performed it seemingly effortlessly doesn't mean his boss shouldn't appreciate how well the job was done. The same goes for you. You want to make sure people know what it takes for you to accomplish all that you do. If they aren't aware of your efforts, they won't appreciate what you did to arrive at the end result.

A director of a small business unit within Amazon.com came to me with this situation: He always waited until his performance review to track accomplishments. He didn't look for opportunities along the way to share the impact he was having. Instead, he sat back and hoped his work would speak for itself. He assumed that senior management knew what he was doing and was aware of his contributions to the company's success. This passive approach did nothing to advance his career or earn him any visibility—something he finally realized when he attended a meeting where his peers were praised for projects for which he had done all of the work. It dawned on him at that moment that senior management wouldn't know what work he was doing or what contributions he was making unless he told them. But how should he go about it?

Our work together allowed him to see how important it is to be proactive. He realized that he has an opportunity every day to sell himself by informing management of the impact he makes on the company. But first he needed to boost his own awareness of his past successes and track his current projects. With his list of accomplishments and action plan in hand, he started to inform influential leaders of what he was doing. They, in turn, began to see the impact he was having and how his work benefited the department. He represented himself in the best way possible, reaping the benefits of his efforts. Colleagues began to praise him openly and offer to help on larger projects. Senior managers chatted with him in the hallway and mentioned him at meetings. As his visibility increased, so did his job satisfaction and his chances of receiving the promotion that would propel his career forward and allow him to become an even stronger member of his company.

Hidden in Plain View

I felt extremely uncomfortable as the focal point, in the spotlight. I really like the behind-the-scenes role, because all my freedom is there.

—Brian Eno
English musician and composer

During my keynote presentation at the Oracle Women's Leadership (OWL) conference, I posed this question to the 200 women in attendance: "How many of you tend to shy away from visibility?" More than half the room raised their hands, which is not an unusual response. Indeed, many of my clients confide that they are afraid to speak up. Kelly P. Finch, an executive vice president at PNC Bank, says that "the risk of me not speaking was far greater than the risk of saying what I thought."[13] People often fear that what they say would open them up to criticism and rejection. A Japanese proverb comes to mind: "The nail that sticks up gets hammered down." Whether speaking up feels unnatural or you simply tend to be a bit shy or hesitant, you still must find ways to be visible, or your career will suffer. Andrea Jung, who oversees 40,000 employees as the chairman and CEO of Avon Products, had to overcome inclinations she'd learned almost since birth. As an individual who was raised in an Asian household, Andrea grew up in a culture that frowned on being assertive. She explains, "When I first went into business, I did have a tough time. It's countercultural for me to be the most energetic person at the meeting. It's countercultural to assert yourself. Through most of my thirties and forties, I had to work on it, to have a seat at the table and have a point of view. I think I have found a sweet spot that feels like I'm still me."[14]

People come from cultures or families that taught them not to speak up, stand out, promote themselves, and create visibility for themselves.

Thomas Jefferson is another example of a remarkable individual who didn't let his introverted, soft-spoken, and shy nature become a hindrance to success. He was described thus: "A tall, slim, quiet man with grey eyes and reddish hair, he could be lively and even vivacious among his friends. But in public he was so reserved, so soft-spoken, and shy, he often seemed stiff or aloof. 'During the whole time I sat with him in the Congress,' said John Adams, 'I never heard him utter three sentences together.'"[15] Jefferson leveraged his talent for writing to become known. Many members of Congress knew him through his writing. He was a tireless writer who wrote over 18,000 letters. Indeed, he made himself so visible that he was selected to write the Declaration of Independence at the young age of 33.

Sometimes, people come from cultures or families that taught them not to speak up, stand out, promote themselves, and create visibility for themselves. For introverts, these issues are prevalent. According to a Harvard Business School article by Carmen Nobel, "Here's the problem: research shows that introverts, not prone to self-promotion, typically have more trouble than their extraverted colleagues rising through the corporate ranks to take a leadership role. This is especially true if they are surrounded by extraverted co-workers, who are likelier to receive promotions because they actively draw attention to themselves—fitting the stereotypes of great leaders."[16]

Even if you do not personally relate to the fear of speaking up, it may be a concern for someone who works with you. The better you are able to understand their plight, the easier it will be to help them minimize the fear they experience from having the spotlight on them.

It's common for people who fear attention to have an internal voice that contemplates the negative. This voice constantly questions their ability and undermines their belief in themselves, therefore making them less likely to speak up. To counter this intense and relenting energy, you need to find specific examples and experiences of how you have actually spoken up with successful results. Stop focusing on the fears and the negative before entering the spotlight, and instead concentrate on what will go well.

The seven suggestions that follow help people manage fear of the spotlight. These tips will ease the process for those who are uncomfortable speaking up and actively gaining visibility. Implement these suggestions proactively. Remember, extraverted people are proven to have an advantage. They are the ones who gain the recognition and promotions that they actually deserve. One recent study on leadership underscores this point: "In a meta-analysis of the relationship between personality and leadership emergence and effectiveness, Judge, Bono, Ilies, and Gerhardt (2002: 765) found that extraversion is 'the most consistent correlate of leadership across study settings and leadership criteria.' Their results indicated that extraverted employees are significantly more likely to (1) emerge as leaders in selection and promotion decisions, and (2) be perceived as effective by both supervisors and subordinates."[17] It's therefore incredibly important to move past any reluctance you have to share your accomplishments with others by doing at least some of the following.

How to Overcome the Fear of the Spotlight

- **SHARE YOUR ACCOMPLISHMENTS THROUGH WRITING.**

  Writing helps you form your thoughts so you can communicate clearly. With e-mail and texting so common nowadays, you can leverage this form of communication to inform others of how the work you are doing directly affects the company. You can use writing to share information about your expertise and express any innovative ideas that you might have. You can even sign up for events or activities that require you to exhibit your writing skills (for example, write articles for the company newsletter, prepare business proposals and reports, submit blog posts, or create and edit marketing and sales materials).

- **WRITE OUT NOTES ON WHAT YOU WANT TO SAY *BEFORE* INTERACTIONS AND EVENTS.**

  Before meetings, one-on-one appointments, and any situation in which you'll share your perspective, take time to create a draft of the specific points that you would like to cover. Preparing ahead of time will help you to relax when the opportunity arises for you to share your accomplishments and contributions.

- **LEARN THE ART OF SMALL TALK.**

  Since the majority of professional situations involve interacting with others, it's important to know how to speak, connect, and build rapport with other people. The odds are that you have countless opportunities to reach out and interact with people who are senior to you. Whether you are at a meeting in which you choose to sit next to your boss's boss or you seek out a senior executive for questions, you want to make a positive impression during these visible moments.

  Create two questions or talking points beforehand so that you're prepared. Ask open-ended questions that help bring out information about the other person, such as: "How is your day going?" "What projects are you working on? How are they going?" "How was your weekend?" These kinds of questions will help you gain insight into your colleagues' personal interests and activities. You of course want to also discuss professional interests. Therefore, before you attend a business meeting with two top executives, come up with two areas to discuss with them that are directly related to a professional project on which they've worked or a personal topic in which they are interested.

- SCHEDULE ONE-ON-ONE MEETINGS.

  You may have an especially difficult time being yourself in a group setting. For this reason, one-on-one scheduled meetings are conducive to effective and comfortable communication. You can schedule meetings with the people who need to know you so that you can create your visibility one person at a time.

- VOLUNTEER FOR COMMITTEES AND GROUPS AT YOUR COMPANY.

  Many companies have committees for which you can volunteer that aren't directly related to your professional duties. Having a non-work-related setting in which you can relax, be yourself, and become acquainted with others is valuable to your visibility. You can approach various colleagues you may not have a chance to know at work.

- LEAD OR COHOST A MAJOR EVENT OR CONFERENCE AT YOUR COMPANY.

  Most of the activities that support organization-wide events take place behind the scenes. As the event organizer, you gain visibility by having your name exhibited as the host or cohost, by making introductions at the actual event, and when others provide recognition for its success.

- **THINK BEFORE YOU SPEAK.**

    Although thinking before you speak means that you may speak less often, it also means that you will think through and articulate your ideas and opinions more clearly. Others will take notice when you do speak, listen intently to what you have to say, and respect your opinions when you share them. Make sure you don't hide out and become stuck thinking and not speaking; this can be easy to do.

Besides these seven tips, a study titled "Reversing the Extraverted Leadership Advantage" offers these suggestions for introverts: "The popular press is replete with suggestions for individuals low in extraversion to 'build on their quiet strength' (Kahnweiler, 2009) by *practicing their public speaking skills*, achieve the 'introvert advantage' (Laney, 2002) by *smiling more frequently*, leverage 'introvert power' (Helgoe, 2008) by *taking breaks and scheduling time to think*, and take their companies from 'good to great' (Collins, 2001) by *being quiet and reserved, but still strong-willed*."[18]

Summary and Action Steps

Before moving on to Chapter 5—where you'll learn the three-step promotion plan that will help you publicize your success—here are the Chapter 4 summary and action steps.

Summary

- *Determine the remarkable thing that you do that helps you stand out from the crowd.* Figure out exactly what you do that is memorable—that makes a lasting impression and captures others' attention.

- *Be visible, or your career will stagnate.* At some point in your career, the hard work and ability that have previously led to promotions and professional success will not be enough. You must therefore fully leverage visibility to continue moving ahead when you come to this stage.
- *To be a leader, you must be visible.* Leadership and visibility need each other. When combined, they make your value known to the most influential individuals in the company.
- *You gain three benefits by focusing on increasing your visibility.* You become more confident and believe in yourself. You're willing to take risks and go beyond your comfort zone. You minimize the fear of failure and are able to maximize and even test your capabilities.
- *Understand how the six levels of visibility progress from "noticed" to "impact."* The visibility progression helps you go from being noticed to having impact. To reach this "impact" level, you must let go of limiting mind-sets that stunt your professional growth.
- *Overcome mind-sets that impede your visibility.* Are you out of sight and thus out of mind? Do you feel that your work should just speak for itself? Does anyone of importance and influence know who you are? Do other people receive the credit for your work? If you fall into any of these categories, you must take initiative and proactively speak up, claim your accomplishments, and make sure others know your value.
- *Consider the two types of people inside a company.* The worker bee and the rooster each have a relationship to visibility. Which one of these do you most relate to?
- *When speaking up feels unnatural, you must find ways to be visible or your career will suffer.* If you fear the spotlight and don't like speaking up, the seven ways to overcome fear

offered in this chapter will greatly benefit you and help you begin to toot your own horn when needed.

Take Action Now

- Schedule time to think about how you can stand out from the crowd. Focus on what you do that is remarkable and distinctive, and that makes a difference to your colleagues and company. Persuade others to take notice of your impressiveness.

- Review a situation in which you made yourself visible that turned out positively. Take notice of how your self-confidence increased during this visibility experience. Realize that with each visible opportunity you choose to take on, your confidence grows.

- Identify an opportunity to increase your visibility that exists right now, and pledge to accomplish this visible task within the next seven days. Overcome any risk-taking fear so you can reap the benefits of being visible.

- Choose something that you know you should be doing to increase your visibility, but are reluctant to act on due to an accompanying fear of failure. Mark on your calendar the date by which you plan to accomplish this task. Ask one person to hold you accountable so you receive the necessary support that will allow you to move past your fear.

- Review the section on "Mind-Sets That Stunt Your Growth," limiting mind-sets with which you operate that affect your visibility. Which is most familiar to you? Create two strategies for how you can overcome this limitation.

- If you are uncomfortable speaking up, review the "How to Overcome the Fear of the Spotlight" section and choose two ways to implement immediately. If you are extremely shy, hesitant, or afraid to speak up, implement two ways per week over the next few weeks to experience the benefits of them all.

- Identify three people who are visible in your organization, and review what they've done to achieve this level of visibility. Write about what it would look like to have this kind of visibility yourself.

5

Promote Your Success

Understand that you need to sell you and your ideas in order to advance your career, gain more respect, and increase your success, influence, and income.

—Jay Abraham
American author and marketing consultant

Three-Step Promotion Plan

Promoting yourself is a necessity for your own—and your company's—future success. In order for you to advance, you *must* make people aware of the benefits you provide to the company. The same is true for an entire organization. When companies know about their employees' talents and assets, they can fully utilize these capabilities.

Your continued career growth and advancement will come naturally as you implement this three-step promotion plan:

1. Self-promote.
2. Promote others.
3. Others promote you.

All three of these areas will directly benefit you. The purpose of self-promotion is to make sure others know what you do and the success you've achieved. Bear in mind that the promoting process must start with you. You have to believe in yourself—what you do, your value—and be willing to share it with others. Let people know the impact you make.

The second step is to promote others. This is done by praising and acknowledging your colleagues' success and achievements. Supporting others in this way allows you to advance, since connecting to another person's success reflects positively back on you. People associate *you* with the success. When your team does well, you do well.

The third step is to have others advocate for you, which they can do only if you've promoted yourself. You must make yourself known through your self-promotion, which will prompt people to notice who you are and the value you offer. You want to provide them with a foundation of success stories and accomplishments to make

> *You have to believe in yourself— what you do, your value—and be willing to share it with others.*

it easier for them to endorse you. *When others speak positively about you, your reputation greatly improves* (see Figure 5.1).

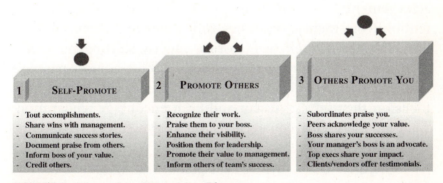

FIGURE 5.1 Three-Step Promotion Plan

Step 1: Self-Promotion—Spread the Word about You

It is important that you recognize your progress and take pride in your accomplishments. Share your achievements with others. Brag a little. The recognition and support of those around you are nurturing.

—Rosemarie Rossetti
American speaker and author

According to Laura Morgan Robert, assistant professor in organizational behavior at Harvard Business School, "People are constantly observing your behavior and forming theories about your competence, character, and commitment. . . . It is only wise to add your voice in framing others' theories about who you are and what you can accomplish."[1]

If you don't add your own voice, you let other people perceive you without having any say in how they see you. You can contribute your voice by letting others know about your accomplishments, thereby making them aware of how valuable you are. Though it might seem a bit awkward at first, don't discourage the attention that comes or be hesitant to take the deserved credit when you're discussing your accomplishments. Author Anne Fels underlines this point in the *Harvard Business Review*: "But far from celebrating their achievements . . . women too frequently seek to deflect attention from themselves. They refuse to claim a central, purposeful place in their own stories, eagerly shifting the credit elsewhere and shunning recognition."[2] This is most people's tendency—to avoid soaking in compliments and keeping the focus on themselves. Accept and even encourage recognition. Take in the credit you receive. Be at the center of success. Bask in its glory.

You must track, identify, and share your accomplishments. Other people must know who you are and the overall impact you make on the company.

Focus on the following elements when tracking your accomplishments:

- Business results.
- The value you've provided to the company.
- Fact-based, concrete details.
- Specific feedback you've received from others.
- Quantifiable data (this is especially persuasive, because it objectively measures the impact of your accomplishments).

Use the accomplishment template provided in Table 5.1 or customize one for yourself. Share it with upper management, your boss, and any advocates. Schedule time right now in your calendar to create an accomplishment list—and don't delay. You will have a situation in the next couple of weeks in which you will wish you had this available to share. To download a blank copy of this form, e-mail me at Joel@GarfinkleExecutiveCoaching.com.

TABLE 5.1 How to Track Your Value to the Organization

	FOCUS ON ACCOMPLISHMENTS	**STATE YOUR IMPACT IN TERMS OF MEASURABLE AND MEANINGFUL RESULTS**
Internal Feedback	Positive comments that colleagues have made about you or your work.	JoAnne told me how impressed she was with the thoroughness and quality of my sales presentation, which resulted in 20 percent increased profit for the company.
Successes	Projects that have been successful. Look at the entire project and break it down into its successful components.	I developed and managed online marketing initiatives and strategies, including webcasts, e-store, and major trade shows to drive profits from $13 million to $18 million.
Outcomes	Positive results that occurred due to your actions.	I created synergy with European and Asia-Pacific marketing/ business development teams to introduce new products to their markets, resulting in 30 percent increased revenue.

(continued)

TABLE 5.1 (*continued*)

	FOCUS ON ACCOMPLISHMENTS	STATE YOUR IMPACT IN TERMS OF MEASURABLE AND MEANINGFUL RESULTS
Bottom-Line Results	Measurable results that underscore the financial impact your accomplishments had on the company.	I increased profits by $450,000 in only four months.
External/Client Feedback	Comments from key clients when you've accomplished something positive for them.	The CIO of XYZ Corporation told me his company saved more than $2 million in inventory costs, thanks to the solution I proposed. He's recommending our services to all of his company's subsidiaries.
Relationships	Enhanced relationships with other business units.	I formed alliances with other business units to improve relations and efficiency between departments. This resulted in seven consecutive quarters of sustained sales growth of 18 percent.
Responsibilities	Responsibilities you have fulfilled for your position, the department, or the company.	I increased product launches by 20 percent by working as liaison with the Sales Department to promote awareness of software solutions among external customers.

A client of mine who is a vice president at Genentech, Inc., tracked his accomplishments on a weekly basis for over a year. He enjoyed the following benefits as a result:

> *As you become increasingly aware of your achievements, you will grow more comfortable telling others specifically how you provide value to the company, which directly alters how they perceive you.*

- Having a ready-made list during review season.
- Keeping front of mind all that he had accomplished. He didn't forget or downplay all that he did.

- Writing the details of the accomplishments while they were fresh in his mind so he didn't lose important and in-depth information.
- Enhanced self-confidence, since the list of accomplishments allowed him to easily see his progress over time.

If you are initially uncomfortable sharing accomplishments, practice with someone. It will become easier each time you do it. Then when you're presented with real situations, you'll find more gumption to deliver an accomplishment you are proud of.

Not only does tracking your accomplishments create concrete examples of your value, but the tracking process itself will give you confidence. As you become increasingly aware of your achievements, you will grow more comfortable telling others specifically how you provide value to the company, which directly alters how they perceive you. They immediately realize your value and your impact on the company due to the results you've achieved.

Find ways to share your accomplishments with others. Write e-mails informing others of your successes. Here is a sample e-mail:

E-mail Subject Line: Thanks for Your Encouragement

Dear Ms. Johnson,

I wanted to let you know that your recent comment in the company e-newsletter really struck a chord with me. I agree that, regardless of one's title here at XYZ Corp., sales should be part of everyone's job. I am a systems programmer in the IT department and don't come into contact with outside customers very often, but I make it a point to look for sales opportunities whenever I can.

For example, I faced a situation two months ago in which several orders for key components to upgrade our mainframes were backlogged. When I talked to our

(continued)

(*continued*)

supplier at ABC Computer Services in New York City, I learned they were having inventory management problems throughout their organization. I realized that one of our XYZ subsidiaries provides consulting services to specifically address inventory management problems like theirs. So I called the divisional sales rep and he contacted my supplier to offer his services. To make a long story short, we solved his inventory problems and generated an additional $150,000 in revenues for XYZ. And now I'm getting my parts on time. So it's a win-win-win for everyone!

Just thought you should know that I took your message about growing our business seriously. Thanks for your comments.

Sincerely,
Brad Thomas
Systems Programmer
XYZ Corp. IT Division

Advocate for Yourself

It's not bragging if you can back it up.

—Muhammad Ali
Former three-time World Heavyweight Boxing Champion

Effective self-promoters realize that there is nothing shameful or improper about seeking credit and recognition for their accomplishments. Having a healthy view of your strengths and being able to convey them to your superiors is neither conceited nor arrogant. You should be proud of what you do, and feel confident in sharing your talents and the impact you have had on the company. Others receive this information from you positively when it comes from a sincere place. In fact, your superiors will appreciate this opportunity to discover your abilities and talents; this allows them to best leverage your role on their team.

In my role as an executive coach with clients at many of the world's leading companies, I've learned that those who advance the furthest and fastest aren't necessarily the most talented or most deserving; however, one quality they almost always share is the ability to *effectively communicate their impact and value* to others in their organizations.

Self-promotion helps create a culture in which people openly and enthusiastically discuss their accomplishments and results. When people reveal this information to each other, they share the best ideas and practices, thereby elevating the entire culture to another level. Employees are able to promote themselves without annoying their superiors or alienating their colleagues.

So how do they do it? And, more important, how can *you*? By applying the following eight suggestions, you'll become noticed and recognized *without* inciting resentment in those around you.

> *Your accomplishments are the currency you use to calculate your value to the company.*

Discuss the Specific Steps of the Accomplishment   Your accomplishments are the currency you use to calculate your value to the company. If you make your accomplishments known, you'll make your value known. Promote the specific steps you took and your precise role in achieving the objective. Make sure you present information in a way that doesn't sound boastful, but discusses your achievement in a way that portrays you positively. The following are some instances in which you can do so.

- Comments from your boss when you've accomplished something positive.

    Example: JoAnne told me how impressed she was with the thoroughness and quality of my sales presentation, which resulted in 20 percent increased profit for the company.

- Projects you've worked on that have been successful. Break the entire project down into its successful components.

  Example: I developed and managed online marketing initiatives and strategies, including webcasts, e-store, and major trade shows to drive profits from $13 million to $18 million.

- Positive results that occurred due to your actions.

  Example: I created synergy with European and Asia-Pacific marketing/business development teams to introduce new products to their markets, resulting in 30 percent increased revenue.

- Responsibilities you have fulfilled for your position, the department, or the company.

  Example: I increased product launches by 20 percent by working as liaison with the sales department to promote awareness of software solutions among external customers.[5]

Take Action Now Review your calendar, e-mails, and projects for indicators. Make a list of everything you've accomplished in the past year, and choose the 10 most powerful or important accomplishments. Try to assign a dollar amount, measurable result, or benefit to the company for each one. Having this list of accomplishments prepared will make you ready to prove your worth to everyone at your organization.

Share Your Achievements and Capabilities with Everyone Jeffrey Pfeffer, a professor at the Stanford University business school, accurately points out, "Don't assume that anyone—your boss, your peer, or your subordinate—knows the good work you are doing. They are all probably focused on their own jobs and concerns. Do things to let them know."[6] Every person with whom you interact at work—including your boss, boss's boss, vendors, clients, peers, senior management, and others—needs to know what you are achieving, the capabilities you offer, and the outstanding skills you possess. Your job is to make sure others see you as adding value and someone who enhances whatever you work on. You're constantly trying to improve your reputation so word will arrive back to the influential players in the organization. You feel empowered when you share your accomplishments and can see how much impact you are actually making. Your confidence grows, as does others' respect for you.

Take Action Now   Make a list of the people with whom you interact directly and indirectly at work—your boss, his/her boss, vendors, clients, peers, and anyone in senior management. Create a table or chart with all the names on the left-hand side. On the right, next to each name, jot down the accomplishment you plan on sharing and then the date once you actually share it. You'll begin to notice how extensively your value is known by others as you implement this exercise.

Focus on How What You've Done Benefits Your Group, Department, or Company   The self-promotion process can often cause you to concentrate on what you've accomplished without giving any thought to how it benefits the company or management. A big picture approach can soften the impression that you care more about furthering yourself than you do about your organization's success. You need to show how what you do benefits other business units, customers, clients, and people above you, below you, and inside your own department. Try to think constantly about how management will value the task you are completing or have just completed. Ask yourself: How can I have people of influence recognize the contribution I just made to the bottom line? Focus on the executive perspective so that you can customize your accomplishments to their preference and point of view.

> *Every person with whom you interact at work needs to know what you are achieving, the capabilities you offer, and the outstanding skills you possess*

Take Action Now   Take a look at all that you've accomplished in the past year by reviewing your performance appraisal, weekly status reports to your boss, and even past successful projects. Evaluate all of this information and jot down how any tasks you've completed specifically help other business units, customers, clients, and people above you, below you, and inside your own department. As you make notes directly related to the big picture impact, you'll notice how much your work affects other parts of the organization.

Create Weekly or Bimonthly Status Report Meetings with Your Boss   Update your boss (and boss's boss) with weekly or bimonthly status reports that specify your accomplishments and what you've done to make progress on the projects you oversee. The meetings are the perfect opportunity to keep higher-ups posted on all that you have achieved and to communicate the impact you make and the value you provide from week to week. Your boss won't wonder how you are doing or be concerned that you aren't being productive and accomplishing important tasks, since these updates will keep him or her abreast of any issues or problems. Your status reports don't have to be thorough and long; in fact, your boss will probably prefer that you keep them short and to the point. Even if they're brief, these updates will keep you at the forefront of important individuals' minds.

Take Action Now   Once you have established a regular day and time for your weekly or bimonthly meetings, the next step is to make sure you are prepared. Twenty-four hours in advance of your one-on-one meeting, send your manager a prepared document that has the following items listed: update from last week's goals, challenges/issues, updates on projects, wins/accomplishments of the week, and agenda for the meeting. This is an excellent way to sprinkle your accomplishments throughout the document.

Give Credit to Others   Self-deprecation and team acknowledgment is self-promotion. Balance out your own self-promotion with the promotion of others. As Harry S. Truman said, "It is amazing what you can accomplish if you do not care who gets the credit." Identify what others have done, and give the appropriate recognition for it. People feel appreciated and motivated when they receive acknowledgment for their efforts, and these efforts help balance out your own self-promotion (see information about promoting others in the next section).

Take Action Now   Make sure to use opportunities like staff meetings, conference calls, and group e-mails to give credit where credit is due. Select someone who has produced excellent work, solved a problem, worked well with others, or taken the initiative on something ahead of time; in fact, choose a deserving individual right now. Then, at your next gathering, give him or her credit and praise in front of others. But be aware that praising in public sometimes needs to be discreet, and might even occasionally not be the best idea. You have to carefully consider the circumstances. If the credit you are sharing causes jealousy or resentment in your group, it's best to temper it and give praise privately.

Share Success Stories That Involve You   Recognition comes when you can translate your work into meaningful, memorable success stories and make these 30-second communications in a concise and clear way. Stating an accomplishment through a compelling story creates a lasting mental picture that other people remember. Higher-ups will want to pass your story along, because you've communicated it in an easily understood way and provided the clear, positive impact. Former Xerox CEO Anne M. Mulcahy describes the importance of stories as follows: "Stories exist at all levels of the corporation. You talk to tech reps and they'll tell you what they did to help turn this company

> *Balance out your own self-promotion with the promotion of others.*

around. Whether it was saving a buck here or doing something different for customers, everyone has a story."[7]

Take Action Now Identify a measurable accomplishment you've achieved recently, and in four to six sentences describe the situation or problem, the action steps you took, and the results you achieved. This level of detail will create the realism necessary to make the story come alive and not seem as though it's merely a one-time, rare achievement. Practice telling this success story to two people this week. The story creates a memorable experience for others to make note of your impact on the company.

Inform Top Management of Your Wins Don't just rely on your boss to share your accomplishments. Make sure to inform his or her boss, members of senior management, and other business unit leaders. Identify the projects that involve these people and find reasons to contact them. You might have a question or problem you're trying to solve, or maybe you possess information they need. Once you are in conversation with them, share the achievements you've realized and explain how these have benefited their part of the organization.

Take Action Now Select a person in top management with whom you would like to share a recent win. This should be someone who has been positively affected by your success. Once you have identified this person, discern his or her current projects and top priorities. You want to couch the discussion of your accomplishment in terms of what is important to your listener so that he or she will receive the information with enthusiasm.

Document Praise from Others When others share verbal or written information (e-mails, texting) praising, acknowledging, or appreciating something you've done, make sure to document it. Keep track of others' positive statements about you so that you can leverage these encouraging opinions as a way to promote yourself. You can use these statements during your performance review or throughout the year at appropriate times. In fact, it's a good idea to document and share this praise throughout the year, and to not always wait for your performance review. Some corporations actually make decisions about promotions, raises, and bonuses three to five months in advance of completing these reviews. You don't want your own point of view omitted from the decision-making process. Instead, make sure that the positive statements others say about you play an important role in your evaluation.

Take Action Now   Review the successful projects or assignments you have worked on over the past few months. Look at all the e-mails involved in the project and identify any praise you've received. Think about past conversations you've had and the positive comments people made to you about the work you accomplished. At the end of the project, cite anything positive that was stated about the major results achieved. Identify and document all of this information.

I find that many of the clients with whom I work are critical of excellent self-promoters. They are angry because these colleagues have advanced faster in their careers even when they aren't as smart or as talented as my clients are. I recommend that my clients stop being critical and judgmental and, instead, learn from these people who have had great success and probably didn't work as hard to advance in the company. You may not like everything that self-promoting individuals do, but you might gain a few tips that could help accelerate your own career path.

Step 2: By Promoting Others, You Promote Yourself

We cannot hold a torch to light another's path without brightening our own.

—Ben Sweetland
Author of *I Will* and *Grow Rich While You Sleep*

Of the three ways to promote your success, promoting others is the easiest. After all, it simply requires that you recognize them in front of people and share something valuable that they've done. Go out of your way to acknowledge others—individual members of your team, your entire team as a whole, people working for you, and people working for other business units.

If you are a manager, promoting others will help improve your relationship with your team. It's vital to make sure that the people who work for and around you feel appreciated. According to the U.S. Department of Labor, the number-one reason people decide to leave their jobs is because they do not feel appreciated. And a Gallup poll cites that 65 percent of workers have received nothing in the way of praise or recognition in the past year. When you start to recognize others, people throughout the organization will take notice and see and acknowledge them for all their hard work. Increased morale and improved performance will ensue, and, ultimately, your entire organization will enjoy a deeper sense of loyalty.

Credit-Sharing Culture

> *The more credit you give away, the more will come back to you. The more you help others, the more they will want to help you.*
>
> —Brian Tracy
> Self-help author

Promoting others helps to establish a credit-sharing culture. David Kelley, founder of design firm IDEO, has created this type of culture for his company. The *McKinsey Quarterly* reports, "One reason IDEO became a renowned innovation firm under David's leadership is that he relentlessly thanks others for making him look good, gives them credit when the company does something great, and downplays his contribution."[8]

> *It's vital to make sure that the people who work for and around you feel appreciated.*

Building a credit-sharing culture begins by emphasizing the need to recognize others' contributions. As you continue to share the credit and appreciate colleagues, you model this kind of behavior for your entire team and encourage them to begin sharing credit with each other. This type of team is one that others notice because of the uplifting support they provide to each other, the outstanding results they enjoy, and the dedication they have to team success. Of course, as your team becomes noticed, so do you.

When a group is happy with you as their leader, they will say great things about you—how wonderful you are to work for, how much you support their actions, and how you recognize the good job they do. This complimentary language will reflect admirably on you. Your team members become your spokespeople, and readily share with passion and excitement all that you do for the group. Their unbridled appreciation will come through as they promote and recognize you.

Promoting others directly helps to enhance both their and your own visibility. As people hear about them, they become more readily noticed and recognized. Their value and talents become known commodities. Others begin to seek them out for their knowledge capital and decision-making skills. As others become confident in them, their responsibilities increase, and as their responsibilities increase, so does the importance of work they are doing. This directly affects you in that you now have more freedom to abandon the day-to-day tasks (which your team is handling) and work on higher-level, big-picture projects that directly affect your own visibility.

Promote Your Team

As a leader, it is vital to inform others how well your team is doing. Promoting your team's accomplishments will help them stand out and become noticed. This will help others see the impact the team is making on the company, something that directly reflects on your leadership abilities. Any compliment you give to your team also indirectly highlights your own accomplishments. The best part is that you can do this without ever needing to say the word *I*. Instead, you make it all about them, which effectively counters the self-promotion you've been doing. This approach balances the *I* by tempering it with the *we* of your team.

Fear of Promoting Others

A lot of people don't spend any time promoting other members of their professional environment. What might be the reasons for this? And is this something *you* avoid? If so, here is a list of common fears that often keep people from promoting others. You might worry that:

- The person you are endorsing will advance more quickly than you.
- Other people will think you have an ulterior motive.
- You simply don't have the time. You would like to, but you aren't making room in your calendar to make it a priority.
- You won't be seen or recognized yourself, because you are spending too much time promoting others.

Benefits of Promoting Others

Don't let these or any other fears stop you from speaking up on your colleagues' behalf, because the benefits greatly outweigh the imagined drawbacks. By actively promoting others, you open up wonderful opportunities to benefit yourself as well. Encouraging your colleagues and team members is a leadership trait that brings the following advantages:

- *The person becomes grateful to you and motivated to do more.* The people you promote will appreciate the effort you've taken and the rewards they have gained by the recognition.

- *You develop a reputation as someone who is generous and likable.* Word spreads that you recognize people's achievements and like to promote others, prompting more people to want to work for you.

- *You're able to add value without much effort.* It takes only a few positive comments, acknowledgments, recommendations, or appreciations to let people know that they—and their work—are valued.

- *You feel pleasant.* It is enjoyable to provide acknowledgment to someone who deserves it; it makes both you and the other person feel good.

- *You'll help people fulfill their potential.* By acknowledging people's talents, skills, and achievements, you see them more favorably than they see themselves. This kind of recognition will thereby help them identify their own possibly unknown talents and abilities. They can begin to realize their full potential when they are able to maximize their gifts and reach their highest levels of greatness.

A client of mine at Bank of America who oversees 25 people was concerned about how little she was promoting others. During her executive coaching session, we identified three top performers whom she wanted to promote. She spent the next month letting these individuals know specifically what they were doing well, and touted their wins to people of influence. As a result, these three people began to feel more confident. They genuinely believed that their boss cared about them, that she wanted them to do well, and that she "had their back," which inspired them to take risks and achieve more. These three people become more motivated, loyal, and productive.

How to Effectively Promote Others

No man becomes rich unless he enriches others.

—Andrew Carnegie
American industrialist and philanthropist

When you speak about another person's impressive accomplishment, it reflects well on you. If you are this person's manager, it shows what you've done indirectly to make this person successful. If you are promoting a peer or someone above you, it shows that you don't want to take all the credit. People come to perceive you as a team player, one who is selfless and focused on others' success. When you give credit for the hard work and results others have achieved, it will reflect favorably on you.

> *When you give credit for the hard work and results others have achieved, it will reflect favorably on you.*

Though some of the following five ideas were touched on in earlier pages, they're summarized here in a way that will help you identify which ones you want to implement.

Recognize the Contributions of Your Team Members   Share the limelight with your colleagues. Use words like *we, our team,* or *our group* instead of *I,* and name names whenever possible: "We couldn't have done it without Shari Montoya"; "Jim Reynolds in accounting helped us on the budget issues."

Copy Your Boss on Recognition Shared with Your Team   When you recognize others for their efforts, accomplishments, and results, make sure you include and copy your boss or even your boss's boss on the related correspondence.

Create Easy and Visible Opportunities for Others to Speak Up and Share   Find opportunities for others to share. Prepare them for specific situations in which they can speak up and become noticed. This makes it easier for them to make themselves visible when you offer your assistance.

Assign Others to Be the Team Leads of Projects or to Represent You at Meetings   Assign others projects or send them to meetings that provide opportunities for visibility. When assigning individuals, be sure to choose the right person and make sure that that person is properly prepared.

Tell Influential and Powerful People the Impact of This Person Promote the value your employee provides to the company. Contact people of influence and highlight how this individual's involvement contributed to a successful end result. Publicizing people allows them to utilize their talents and skills to their fullest. The company as a whole benefits when it gains more from its employees, and people of influence will recognize ways to leverage these underutilized people.

Step 3: Get Others to Advocate for You

Strong performers should expect their bosses to advocate for them and help them up the ladder.

—Kerry Clark
Former vice chairman of Procter & Gamble

Which product are you more likely to buy: the one the manufacturer says is great or the one your friend recommends? Much like the recommended product, people see you in an extremely favorable light when someone advocates on your behalf. This is a powerful and direct way to increase your visibility and value. An advocate speaks positively in your favor, and makes strong and clearly defined cases for why you are valuable.

> *People see you in an extremely favorable light when someone advocates on your behalf.*

Advocates speak publicly and on positive terms about:

- Impact you are having at work.
- Value you are providing.
- Key ways you are making the people around you better.
- How you are improving the company's bottom line.
- Accomplishments you've realized.
- Ways you reach out and help others.

You Need to Ask

You get in life what you have the courage to ask for.
—Oprah Winfrey
American actress, talk show host, and producer

I'm often surprised by how many of my executive clients don't have others promoting on their behalf. I've always wondered why this is, and have come to the fairly simple conclusion that people just don't ask. If you want others to advocate for you, you have to ask. After all, people typically won't do or say anything on your behalf unless you ask them to or inform them that you actually need this.

So why *don't* people ask? The reason is usually because they aren't comfortable requesting that another person promote them. My clients often say things like "I don't want to take up their time. What if they say no? What if they feel that I don't deserve it or don't have anything positive to say? Maybe they see too many negatives and won't want to speak up on my behalf."

The reason advocates sometimes resist speaking up for another person is because they are concerned about their own reputation, which they put on the line the minute they speak positively to others about you or someone else. This isn't a problem if your actions are positively perceived. If, however, you do something that undermines your performance or makes you look bad, it's a direct reflection on the advocate. You must make sure

> *The more frequently people share about how well you are doing, the better your reputation becomes.*

you are a star employee with whom people *want* to associate. Impress others with your demeanor and abilities, and make them feel as though it's easy to say good things to others about you. Establish and develop relationships with people so they know you; this will help build trust and, in turn, make it easier for them to advocate on your behalf.

Types of People Who Can Advocate for You

Few people are successful unless other people want them to be.
—Charlie Brown
Peanuts cartoon character

The more frequently people share about how well you are doing, the better your reputation becomes.

Here are seven types of people who can advocate for you:

1. *People working above you.* This group is an ideal choice because of the amount of weight their point of view carries. These senior people can come from within your group as well as from other business units.
2. *Your boss's boss.* This is someone who might know you fairly well, but who will not be as biased as your direct boss might be. The boss's boss has more influence, and his or her opinion will therefore have more impact.
3. *Your immediate boss.* Your immediate boss has definite power when promoting you because he or she knows you well, has direct experience working with you, and speaks from a place of authority. Any impressive stories and examples your boss shares can positively shape your reputation.

When your boss is respected and influential, his or her opinion carries extra weight. The downside occurs, however, when your boss has less influence, and therefore less impact. Further, the authenticity of your boss's words might be diminished if others perceive him or her as biased due to a close relationship with you.

4. *Your peers.* Believe it or not, your peers' opinions can sometimes convey more impact than your boss's, since peers don't work for you and you don't work for them. They have an informal dotted line to you, a nonobligatory relationship that makes for unbiased opinions. Coworkers can often state honestly what they see, which causes their opinions to matter more to others. It's especially vital to have peers who are highly respected by people of influence positively speak up on your behalf.

5. *People below you.* Individuals who work below you make a solid impression on others when they speak about you. Because they aren't expected to say anything at all, it carries impact—and a little bit of surprise—when they do. This is helpful because it enhances your reputation and reflects positively on you. Even though they might have little influence in the overall organization, their opinion still holds weight and can add to a strong overall impression of you.

6. *Your clients or customers.* Clients are a special group because they operate outside the organization. All companies who value their clients and customers understand their importance and bend over backward to make sure they are happy. Their opinion *matters*. So when clients advocate for you, it makes a bold statement. Ask clients with whom you have a good rapport to speak up on your behalf by writing about what they appreciate, and then sharing this with your management. You can explain the impetus behind your request: that management isn't fully aware of the work you are

doing, and you're attempting to make more people at your company cognizant of your contributions. If you do this four to six times a year, it will influence how management views you in a very favorable way.

7. *Vendors, suppliers, and product development partners.* The vendor or supplier is another individual who is outside the organization and can therefore provide a different understanding of the benefits you offer. Leveraging outsiders as advocates, as you would with clients or customers, can provide a positive and unique perspective.

Taken together, the members of these seven groups give a complete picture of you and a solid amount of feedback to make the right impression to others.

When the Boss Doesn't Advocate

What happens if you have a boss who, for one reason or another, doesn't actively promote your accomplishments? I've heard many coaching clients say, "I've become invisible because my boss doesn't update anyone on what we are doing as a team or individually." In cases like these, I've advised clients to send an accounting of their accomplishments to important and influential people without undermining their boss's authority. Copy your immediate boss on the e-mail updates and explain beforehand why you feel this step is necessary. Your reasons should focus on the benefits to the company, inclusivity with other departments, and the wide impact of your work.

One way of doing this is to send detailed and value-added updates on the projects you're working on and describe your direct involvement in their success. Make sure that you emphasize the impact these have had on the company. Before sending the update, discuss how this information benefits the people receiving it; in other words, don't just send random updates. If these people gain value from what they receive, they will be inclined to appreciate it. You end up adding value directly to them. The updates will help others see you as an expert and go-to person on whom they can rely.

Eight-Step Process to Create Advocates

If you want advocates, follow the eight steps shown in Table 5.2.

Step 1: Make Yourself Visible Being visible is vital to having others promote you. After all, if they don't know who you are, they won't be willing to advocate for you. Visibility is about becoming noticed and seen. Once you've done so, you are ready

TABLE 5.2 Eight-Step Process to Create Advocates

Step 1	Make Yourself Visible
Step 2	Demonstrate Your Value
Step 3	Find Advocates
Step 4	Ask People to Advocate for You
Step 5	Explain Why You Need an Advocate
Step 6	Show the Benefit for the Advocate
Step 7	Create a One-Sheet Talking Point Document
Step 8	Follow Up to Make Sure Advocates Are Promoting You

to show your value to the company. Here are a couple of ideas to promote your own visibility:

- Write a one-paragraph, timely e-mail simply stating (in a nonboastful way) how what you accomplished helped a situation, problem, or project.
- Ask a client to pass along the good news when you've solved a problem or provided excellent customer service.

Step 2: Demonstrate Your Value   Others need to see and know your value. When you share accomplishments, be sure to attach value to why they are important. Each result you achieve needs to entail what you did and the impact it has had on the company, your business unit, or other divisions. Constantly evaluate and ensure you are delivering more value and profit than you previously have.

Demonstrating your value comes from focusing on areas such as money saved, money earned, time saved, enhanced efficiency, reduction of expenses, improved retention, increased staff morale, higher profitability, better customer service, improved sales, improved time to market, achieved financial goals, increased stakeholder involvement, identified new opportunities for growth, increased productivity, and improved leadership effectiveness. (See the self-promotion section of this chapter for more information.) When you demonstrate your value, people will see how the tasks you accomplish at work produce something necessary and needed. They will see the importance of everything you do.

Step 3: Find Advocates   As previously stated, there are seven types of advocates, and you want all seven to actively advocate for you. They need to speak up about you publicly in flattering terms. Create a list of all the advocates from whom you

> *Forge connections with mentors, peers, and powerful people who can help you blow your own horn—or blow it for you.*
>
> —Anne Fels

can choose; ideally, this will be at least 10 people. You might be surprised with some of the names you come up with here; a lot of advocates are sitting right in front of you and you don't even know it. You've never asked them to speak on your behalf, and they've never offered. Choose advocates who are respected, have influence, and will say something of importance. Make sure they are individuals to whom others look for guidance and to make key decisions.

Step 4: Ask People to Advocate for You   Advocates won't promote another person unless they are asked, since they don't know you need it. You must forge connections and do as Anne Fels in the *Harvard Business Review* article "Do Women Lack Ambition?" suggests: "In itself, high-caliber work won't generate proper recognition for your accomplishments. Forge connections with mentors, peers, and powerful people who can help you blow your own horn—or blow it for you."[9] Almost all advocates say yes when asked. The moment that you ask them, you make yourself visible to them. You put yourself front and center, so they now look at you differently. They take an interest in you and your success, and become invested in and want to help you.

Everything you do at work affects at least one person on your advocate list. Whether it's the people working above you, your boss's boss, your immediate boss, your peers, the people below you, or clients and vendors—your work touches all of them. Keep your eyes open to the ways that every one of your achievements actually benefits your advocates. Then connect these to a way that they can speak up on your behalf. If something you do helps one of them, ask that advocate to acknowledge your contribution publicly. If you have a huge win on a project, make sure your boss shares the news with senior management, and explains exactly how it benefited the company.

Step 5: Explain Why You Need an Advocate   Advocates don't know why you need them to speak positively on your behalf, so you often have to explain your situation. Be sure to make such points as:

- Few people, if any, know about or have recognized the excellent work you've been producing.
- You haven't had a promotion in years and it's well deserved.
- You receive positive and enthusiastic comments from individuals that no one else knows about.
- You help mentor, support, and grow others, but don't believe that anyone perceives this.
- You are influential, but few people see the connection between your influence and the outcomes.

Make sure you explain why you want them to be advocates and share with others the impact you've made. You are leveraging advocates to understand your plight and speak up on your behalf. When your boss or boss's boss isn't effective at promoting you, it's up to you to gain other advocates to take your side.

Step 6: Show the Benefit for the Advocate   The person you're asking is probably wondering why he or she should advocate for you. The first reason is that it feels good to speak positively about another person. Second, it provides advocates with the opportunity to simultaneously promote themselves, continually demonstrating the valuable effect they are having on the organization, which, in turn, enhances their own reputation. Gently inquire about times when advocates spoke up on *their* behalf and how it may have positively influenced their own career. Ask your potential advocate how it felt to have someone act as a champion—and how good it would feel to do the same!

Step 7: Create a One-Sheet Talking Point Document for the Advocate   Your one-sheet talking point document should list the numerous accomplishments that summarize your value to the organization. These talking points make it easy for your advocate to be your spokesperson. You can design this sheet with three columns. The first one should list general areas, the second one specifies your accomplishments, while the third demonstrates the result and impact for each. Share this document with your advocates so they can use it to champion your success. See an example of this in the self-promotion section (Table 5.1, "How to Track Your Value to the Organization").

Step 8: Follow Up to Make Sure Advocates Are Promoting You
Even though you have worked hard to arrange for advocates to speak up on your behalf, promoting you may not be top of mind for them, given all the other responsibilities they have. So follow up with them on a regular basis to make sure it stays a priority and is completed at your level of satisfaction.

Each time you receive a compliment, achieve a result, or provide something of value, you should let your advocates know and ask them to share with others what you have done. This request can be made via e-mail or voice mail or, even better, in person. The stronger the case you make for your advocates' support at that juncture, the less you need to follow up. Once someone has agreed to advocate for you about a particular accomplishment, check in with him or her within 48 hours and ask if the request has been completed. If you don't follow up, there is a higher chance that your request will be lost.

Summary and Action Steps

In Chapter 6, you'll be reading about the importance of becoming visible by speaking up often and increasing your visibility at meetings. You'll be learning the four different personalities that show up in your relationship to visibility. Before moving ahead, however, here are the Chapter 5 summary and action steps.

Summary

- *Promote your success.* There are three ways to promote your success: self-promotion, promoting others, and having others promote you. All three of these areas benefit both the company and yourself. The company gains the most from your efforts, and you achieve continued success and advancement.

- *Add your own voice to positively frame what others think about you.* Adding your voice comes from communicating your accomplishments so others know how valuable you are.

- *Self-promotion has a bad reputation.* Learn the art of self-promotion so you can use it to your advantage. If you don't self-promote effectively, your work goes unnoticed and your career will suffer.

- *There are many benefits and advantages to promoting others.* Promoting others directly helps to enhance both their and your own visibility. Recognizing your colleagues and associates in front of people helps others appreciate the value of what they've done. By promoting others habitually, you help to develop the kind of credit-sharing culture that benefits all members.

- *Get others to advocate for you.* Having others speak on your behalf enhances your reputation and improves people's perception of you. Advocates make strong and clearly defined cases for why specific people are valuable. Don't wait for people to speak up on your behalf; ask others to serve as advocates.

- *There are seven types of people who can become an advocate for you.* These are people working above you, your boss's boss, your immediate boss, your peers, people below you, your clients or customers, and vendors, suppliers, and product development partners. You must ask these people to advocate for you; you can't wait for them to come to you or for it to happen naturally.
- *Follow the eight-step process to create advocates.* This involves the following: Make yourself visible, demonstrate your value, find advocates, ask them to advocate for you, explain why you need an advocate, show the benefit for the advocate, create a one-sheet talking point for the advocate, and follow up to make sure advocates are promoting you.

Take Action Now

- Review the list of ways to effectively self-promote, and choose one to practice each day during the next two weeks (you may want to or need to work on some points for more than one day). You will have completed all eight strategies at the end of the two weeks; your ability to self-promote will feel easier, and you'll notice immediate results.
- Recognize others' contributions. Schedule time this week to complete each one of these tasks: Choose a person on your team to acknowledge, compliment one of your direct reports, and share an accomplishment from one of your subordinates to an influential person in another business unit.
- Reread the "How to Effectively Promote Others" section and choose two tactics (out of the five) to implement over

the next three weeks. Notice how applying these five tips helps people perceive you as a team player who is focused on others' success.

- Review the many different types of people who can advocate for you, and choose which one(s) you want to advocate for you. Ask these individuals to speak on your behalf, and provide details on what you want them to do.
- Go through the "Eight-Step Process to Create Advocates" right now. Don't delay; they are waiting to hear from you.

6

Speak Up, Speak First, and Speak Often

To produce results, visibility must be combined with credibility. This means that you need to embrace visibility strategies that display your distinction, competence, expertise, authority, and leadership.

—Steven Van Yoder
American journalist and author

Different Levels of Visibility

We're all aware of the fact that every person is different, and who we are and how we show up at work are unique. People come from different families, genders, races, classes, and cultures. These variances influence your professional behavior, the approach you bring to certain situations, and your overall comfort regarding visibility. All of these elements either enhance or limit your success at work.

Based on who you are, you will likely identify with one of these four types of personalities as they relate to visibility. Which one are you?

1. *Observer*—Stands back, observes, and holds back from visibility.
2. *Participant*—Becomes visible when comfortable.

3. *Initiator*—Actively looks for and creates visibility.
4. *Leader*—Is influential and maintains high visibility.

It may be easy for you to quickly identify with one predominant personality type, a couple of different types, or all four of these roles based on the circumstances in which you find yourself. Whatever type you are, the ultimate objective is to become a *leader* and to maintain high visibility. Even individuals with *observer* or *participant* tendencies have to learn and leverage how to stand out and make themselves known. The *leader* is who you need to become to maintain the competitive advantage necessary in today's work environment.

Being visible doesn't always feel natural for *observers* and *participants*. These individuals prefer to stay in their comfort zones and not rock the boat. The reluctance to become visible, however, can severely limit potential career growth. When you are not visible, you are *in*visible. You cannot expect to make a difference, let alone get promoted, if you are invisible.

Everything you're learning about visibility provides a catalyst to make change. When you follow the steps and ideas outlined in Part Two of this book, you'll become the influential *leader* you were meant to be.

Observer

The observer is someone who has interest in the content of others' interactions, but lacks personal involvement. Observers aren't vocal. They silently observe by taking in and digesting information. They tend to watch what is happening without much participation.

There are usually three types of observers. One chooses to not speak up because he has nothing to actually say or add to a situation. He is content with his role as observer and doesn't feel any need to change it, except

> *When you are not visible, you are invisible.*

when he realizes how much it undermines his career due to the lack of visibility.

Another type of observer is one who doesn't speak up because she fears what others might think of her. This person *isn't* fine just observing; she wants to overcome this fear and be able to participate in conversations. She knows she has insights to share and knowledge to add that could be helpful. But her fear is so great that she holds everything inside.

The third type is the shy person who dances between both of the first two types. He would like to speak up at times, but feels incredibly uncomfortable doing so. His reservations are less about fear of what others think and more about his tendency to be an introvert. The whole concept of visibility is too confrontational for his personality.

Whatever the reasons, all three types of observers don't speak up. They don't become recognized and known inside the company, which substantially damages their visibility.

Being an observer does have its benefits. These people take in and assimilate all information; therefore, when they do speak, they usually share well-thought-out and articulate comments. Observers often command more attention when they talk, because it's so rare to hear them speak up. This can cause others to listen closely and really hear what that person is saying.

The major challenge that observers face is that their reluctance to speak up means that fewer people will know them. They can become caught in continuous observation mode and fail to share in the conversation in any way—and they might start to feel safe in this mode. No one will judge or question them as long as they remain quiet. Unfortunately, no one will know what they have to offer, either.

Participant

Participants want to share a lot of information and knowledge and to speak up actively whenever they can. They're eager to reveal what they know. They see situations in which it would be beneficial for them to speak up; however, they often don't. Even when they're interested in the subject matter being discussed, they're reluctant to ask questions or engage in conversations.

This is because participants are willing to make themselves visible *only when comfortable* with the person, situation, or group setting. As long as the conditions seem safe, they feel comfortable enough to share. For participants, the most vital factor to sharing is trust, which comes only when they know the environment or people involved. When participants feel secure, they're comfortable speaking up. If a new situation arises, however, sharing becomes difficult.

Being a participant does have its benefits. Participants genuinely want to share. They will speak up with ease and confidence when the situation is right for them. They might even surprise people with the amount they do communicate when they are comfortable. Like observers, they come across as articulate when they do share something, because they have had time to formulate their thoughts.

The biggest hurdle for participants is the hesitancy involved with actually speaking up. Once they overcome this fear and begin speaking, they are able to share their opinions quite effectively. While observers never completely feel comfortable sharing, participants become at ease once they begin doing so. This is one advantage the participant has over the observer, and it's also one reason why people are surprised with how composed participants can seem once they begin sharing. They are able to create visibility and let others know who they are as they converse more and more. The hardest part for the participant is simply to *begin*.

Another major challenge for participants is the lack of visibility. Not enough people know the participant. When people finally hear them speak up, it provides only a limited impression of who they are and the imprint they have on the company. This isn't enough for others to form a comprehensive understanding of a participant's value.

Both the observer and the participant feel comfortable speaking when they have their facts together and complete knowledge of the situation. They feel capable, confident, and safe, but people with these personality types stay in the background and receive less visibility.

Initiator

The initiator actively looks for and creates visibility. Nothing holds initiators back; they are all about being visible and becoming known. They know how to be seen and appreciated, and aggressively apply themselves toward becoming noticed. As such, they will do the new and unexpected to be visible. They know full well that they can create the exact reputation they desire.

Initiators don't wait for others to notice them. They proactively involve themselves by taking actions that lead others to know who they are. They aren't afraid to speak up or share.

Initiators will start a conversation with the same ease with which they jump right into an already-established discussion. They do not shy away from challenging conversations, nor do they hesitate to address any issues or problems. This tendency helps grow their visibility. Initiators will speak up to anyone, regardless of the person's status, level of influence, or power.

Initiators benefit in being seen and having others readily notice their talents and abilities. Their efforts and success are frequently recognized and validated. Initiators create their own visibility and don't have to rely on others to do it for them. The influential people inside the organization know who the initiators are and seek them out for desirable projects. Being an initiator provides a solid foundation for the move toward becoming a *leader*.

The initiators' challenge is to know when to turn down or even turn off their proactive desire for visibility. They are so focused on making themselves known that it can actually cause them to make poor decisions. Sometimes they create visibility at the expense of others; they can become too noticed and offend colleagues or managers. Their confidence can seem like arrogance, and they can become overly outspoken or obnoxious when sharing their opinions.

Leader

The leader works on maintaining the high visibility that he or she has established. While observers, participants, and initiators spend their time seeking visibility, the leader doesn't have to because he or she has already gained it. Leaders are under enormous pressure, however, to continue to produce important results at an extremely high-profile level.

Leaders take on challenging projects and situations. They know full well the risk involved and have the confidence to believe they'll enjoy a positive outcome. Any doubt they have is wrapped in self-assuredness. They accept doubt as part of the process and don't let it limit them in producing results. Because they experience continued success, leaders gain the necessary confidence to maintain high visibility. Even when this exposure leads to extreme pressure, the leader still wants to take it on.

Leaders take risks and do what others are less inclined to do. They want to make themselves known by being the people who won't buckle under the weight of the situation. No matter how overwhelming the circumstances, others perceive the leader as someone who has what it takes to accomplish necessary tasks. Leaders make suggestions, give recommendations, and ask questions that no one else raises or considers. They have a strategic mind-set that differentiates them from others, and are willing to initiate tasks and projects that have never before been attempted. They are able to work through any hesitancy to lead and propel themselves into action. Though they often have no idea how situations will turn out, they always believe in themselves. When things go well, their visibility is off the charts. Others are impressed and even in awe of these people. This is how they maintain high visibility and constant positive recognition from others.

The benefit of being a leader is the amount of constant visibility generated over time, which provides a solid reputation and deep respect from others. People know that they can count on this leader, and that he or she will deliver. Another advantage is that people look to leaders to take charge. They are sought after for their management abilities and are therefore constantly guiding others.

The challenges of being a leader include the tremendous amount of pressure that comes from this high degree of visibility. Leaders are constantly in the spotlight, responding to excessive demands and intense situations. They are faced with countless make-or-break decisions. While they feed off of this pressure, it's relentlessly challenging. Leaders rarely have time to relax. They keep taking risks and choosing to take on the challenging projects, because that is what others expect of them.

What Role Do You Play?

Which one of the four visibility personality types describes you best? Where do you most commonly find yourself?

- Are you an *observer* who watches what's happening and usually doesn't speak up? Do you stand back and refrain from talking until you have gathered all the facts? Do you participate so infrequently that it hinders your visibility and undermines your career?

- Are you a *participant* who wants to share and knows you should, but you often hold yourself back instead? Do you only contribute in safe situations, speaking up only when comfortable (even though that's not enough)? Do you notice others advancing faster than you due to their enhanced visibility by making themselves known and valued within the company?

- Are you an *initiator* who works hard at becoming noticed, standing out, and making others aware of who you are? Do you notice how you constantly speak up and share what you know? Are you constantly making yourself heard and visible to the influential people? Do others seek you out for important projects and recognize you as a potential future leader? Do you ever find yourself speaking up more than others do and perhaps coming across as too outspoken with your opinion? You might even be offending others with your unedited comments.

- Are you a *leader* who focuses on maintaining the high visibility you've already established? Do you feel some pressure at this level, but notice how you are still able to produce solid performance and results? Does your confidence continue to shine with each successful risk you take?

Even though you may find yourself in one category more frequently, different circumstances and situations can place you in any one of the other three categories. For example, consider which visibility personality type you are when you are with:

- Members of your own gender at work.
- Members of the opposite gender at work.
- Your boss.
- Someone in top management.
- A group.
- People who intimidate you.
- Subordinates.
- Someone younger.
- Someone older.
- People you don't know.

- Your family.
- Your spouse.
- Friends.

Whether you naturally tend to lead, initiate, participate, or observe, it should be clear to you that speaking up is vital for your professional success. The next section covers the importance of voicing your opinion. You'll also learn how to increase your visibility at meetings so that others will notice and remember you.

Speak Up, Speak First, and Speak Often

Every time you have to speak, you are auditioning for leadership.
—James C. Humes
American author and presidential speechwriter

Two studies conducted by Cameron Anderson and Gavin J. Kilduff in 2009 found that people who speak up and act dominant will be *perceived* as competent even if they aren't. They merely appear so because they believe so completely in their own competence.

So what does this teach us? Speak up. Speak first. Speak often. Stop overthinking and delaying what you want to say. Stop being fearful; instead, trust in yourself. Have confidence in your knowledge. Focus more on what you know and less on what others think. People want to hear what you have to say. As Abraham Lincoln once said, "It is the man who does not want to express an opinion whose opinion I want." It is time for you to begin sharing your opinion.

> *People who speak up and act dominant will be* perceived *as competent even if they aren't.*

The Anderson and Kilduff study tells us that you don't need to be the most competent leader—you can simply ensure that others perceive you as competent by taking two specific actions:

1. Speak first.
2. Speak more often.

How often do you have something worth sharing, but for whatever reason, you just don't share it? What happens is that the second before you're about to utter that statement, your brain tells you not to. It's often based on a fear of failure or of judgment from others. Over the years, I've had client after client make excuses like these for not speaking up:

- "I'm scared I might say something wrong."
- "I worry that others will see me as incompetent."
- "I'm not important enough to state my opinion."
- "Another person already shared what I wanted to say."
- "I don't want to interrupt."
- "I'm too young; I don't have enough experience."
- "No one will listen."
- "I will say something incorrect, be judged negatively, and cause others to form an inaccurate opinion about me."
- "I'll wait to share my thoughts with people one-on-one."

These fears almost never come to fruition, which is exactly why they must not keep you from speaking up. Your opinion matters; you must be a part of the conversation. In his book *Only the Paranoid Survive*, Andy Grove informs readers, "Your time for participating is now. You owe it to the company and you owe it to yourself. Your criterion for involvement should be that you're heard and understood."[1]

Consider the results of the Anderson and Kilduff study again. They show that you likely will *not* be perceived as incorrect or inaccurate if you speak up at meetings. Instead, you'll be seen as a competent leader if you speak up and speak often. Anderson and Kilduff back up this point by emphasizing, "More-dominant individuals achieved influence in their groups in part because they were *seen* as more competent by fellow group members."[2]

So give yourself permission and freedom to speak up. Anyone who holds back from speaking up in front of groups (which is one of the best ways to create visibility) should realize that they don't have to be perfect or have the one right answer. You don't have to make the smartest or most important contribution. You can speak and be wrong. What matters is that you are heard and heard often. Even if you tend to be a listener, make sure that you force yourself to speak up at least every once in a while. Julie Daum, who is the practice leader for the North American Board Services Practice of *Spencer Stuart*, explains, "People write off people who don't speak. If you don't take up a little bit of airtime, people will assume you have nothing to contribute."[3] Your ability to speak up will cause others to perceive you as a respected leader, which can only enhance your reputation.

Too often, we hold ourselves back because we haven't completely formulated our thoughts. You probably believe that you can't contribute until you're able to communicate clear, well-thought-out ideas. You prefer speaking from a place of depth and clarity. The problem with this approach is that it causes people to overthink. You become stuck inside your thoughts, trying to refine your statements, and you miss the chance to share your—albeit imperfect—comment. Instead of becoming trapped in this cycle of overanalysis, speak up often by sharing surface information, ideas, and questions. This will help you stay engaged in the conversation.

One client of mine at Apple had a habit of hesitating before speaking at meetings. The fact that she was not the first speaker made her hesitate even more, because she felt as though others had already expressed what she wanted to say. We tackled this situation by agreeing that she would share her opinions regardless of whether someone else had already voiced something similar. Even saying something like, "I agree with Jim because . . ." shows a greater degree of engagement than merely sitting there.

> *People write off [other] people who don't speak. If you don't take up a little bit of airtime, people will assume you have nothing to contribute.*
>
> —Julie Daum

And what if you want to disagree? You owe it to yourself, your coworkers, and your company to speak up. As one *Harvard Business Review* article states, "Minority viewpoints have been proven to aid the quality of decision-making in juries, by teams, and for the purpose of innovation. Research first published in the *Journal of Applied Psychology* shows that even when the minority points of view are wrong, they cause the rest of the group to think better, to create more solutions, and to improve the creativity of problem solving."[4]

People tend to discount themselves. Don't underestimate the value of what you have to say or diminish your own value. You need to take the risk to be one of those people who do share. Remind yourself of your capability and knowledge. You know what you are talking about; otherwise, you wouldn't be in *your* position. Others believed in you enough to help you reach the level you're at; now it's time for *you* to believe it.

People need—and want—to hear what you have to say. At every meeting you attend, topics will come up on which you have experience and expertise. These are the ideal situations in which to speak up and add value. Don't waste these opportunities. Take a cue from Ursula Burns, CEO of Xerox Corporation and the first African American to lead a Fortune 500 company. After the announcement that she had become president, she told a reporter, "My perspective comes in part from being a New York black lady, in part from being an engineer. I know I'm smart and have opinions worth being heard."[5]

Don't Wait for Permission to Speak Up at Meetings

I was constantly pushed to find out what I really thought and then to speak up. Over time, I came to see that waiting to discover which way the wind was blowing is an excellent way to learn how to be a follower.
—Roger Enrico
Former CEO of PepsiCo Inc. and current chairman
of DreamWorks Animation SKG Inc.

The average employee spends over one-third of his or her workweek in meetings. That means if you want to be visible, meetings are the best opportunity you have, so take advantage of them. Meetings are the best place to show who you are, and the perfect chance to display your knowledge and expertise. Others learn the value you bring to the organization. As your visibility develops at meetings, influential people will take notice—and these are the people who can help escalate your professional success.

A senior manager at the Starbucks corporate office came to me because he felt that his colleagues didn't recognize the value he brought to the company. His quiet nature and passive style interfered with his need to be visible, especially at meetings that higher-level executives attended. As a result, senior staff members and other influential people had no idea how valuable he really was. It was clear that he needed to become more visible.

The reason my client didn't speak up more was because he was afraid that he might not be accepted if he disagreed publicly with other people in the room. He was afraid to make a mistake or say something inaccurate. So he avoided creating greater exposure for his ideas and gave his power away to other people by assuming that their viewpoints held more weight than his own. He allowed himself to speak only when he knew he had something useful to say and that his comments would be met with approval. He put constant pressure on himself to be careful about what he said and how he said it—and he became overly vigilant about how others received his comments. His fear of conflict prevented him from sharing his opinions, and thus limited his visibility. He needed to learn how to disagree effectively in meetings so that he could speak up without worrying about the consequences. As we worked together, my client learned that speaking up often in meetings would yield two immediate benefits:

1. His ideas and points of view immediately created positive buzz and feedback.
2. He triggered a valuable exchange of ideas in the company.

These benefits, in turn, increased both his and his company's knowledge capital. His enhanced visibility helped him develop more (and deeper) relationships with colleagues and executives in the company. The methods that helped my client better express himself helped boost his visibility as well.

How to Be Visible at Meetings

Our lives begin to end the day we become silent about things that matter.

—Martin Luther King Jr.
American clergyman and civil rights leader

The following are some easy-to-implement tactics for expressing yourself fully in meetings:

- **BELIEVE IN YOUR IDEAS AND HAVE CONFIDENCE IN SHARING THEM.**

    Your ideas are no less valid than those of the other meeting attendees; so don't allow doubt to get in the way of your participating. You do not need to adjust your viewpoint to suit others' needs. When you believe in your ideas, your confidence will expand, and you will in turn find it easier to share your thoughts and ideas.

- **STOP CENSORING YOURSELF.**

  Once you stop censoring yourself, you'll automatically speak more often. It's important to share your thoughts and ideas without overediting them or limiting your expression. Don't lose valuable opportunities to share your views and to be seen as the influential person you are.

- **SAY WHAT FIRST COMES INTO YOUR HEAD.**

  Speak when you want to speak, without hesitation, and not just when you have something seemingly important to say. Commit to expressing one idea that pops into your mind. Practice doing this at least once per meeting so that it becomes a habit. Your newfound ability to jump into a conversation without preparation will soon override any lingering fears. Imagine being the verbose person in the meeting. Yes, that might be a bit radical, but push the limits of your comfort zone. Wouldn't it be powerful not to censor yourself at all? Give yourself the gift of total freedom of expression, and you will soon be comfortable sharing yourself without hesitation.

- **CHOOSE A TOPIC AHEAD OF TIME.**

  Prior to every meeting, choose one topic or agenda item that you will address, even if your perspective is contrary to the prevailing opinion, possibly confrontational, or even a potentially moot point. Select a topic that is important to you and prepare in advance so that you will be ready to add to the discussion.

- **ASK QUESTIONS.**

  One of the easiest ways to speak up in a meeting is to ask questions. Leverage your knowledge and expertise by probing more deeply into what others are saying. You will feel engaged and become an active participant, which will help facilitate a powerful meeting and provide opportunities for others to truly see you. There is no such thing as a dumb question; the only dumb question is the one not asked.

- **DECIDE HOW OFTEN YOU WANT TO SPEAK IN A MEETING.**

  Before each meeting, decide how many times you want to speak, so that you have a target that motivates you to participate. You can, for example, choose to speak three times and let the first be a comment you prepare in advance. The second could be a question you ask, and the third time might be a thought that comes to mind at any point during the meeting.

- **REMIND YOURSELF OF THE SPEAKING-UP SITUATIONS THAT RESULTED IN A POSITIVE EXPERIENCE.**

  Come up with three or four specific times when your participation led to positive results. As you review your list, you'll notice that the outcome actually is positive *every* time you speak up. This will help grow your confidence substantially, and will encourage you to keep sharing.

- **LEVERAGE THESE CLEVER WAYS TO COMFORTABLY COMMUNICATE GOOD IDEAS.**

  In her article "How to Interject in a Meeting," author Jodi Glickman offers four ways to share good ideas when you are unsure of yourself.[6] Simply complete the sentence after these four kickoff phrases as I've done with the following examples:

  1. *Have we thought about* . . . getting Steve involved in the PR campaign directly?

  2. *Did anyone mention* . . . the Brealy report? I seem to recall it covered some of the same topics Andrew has raised here.

  3. *Another option we may want* to *consider* . . . is pushing back the time line until early October.

  4. *Is it worth revisiting* . . . last week's minutes from the meeting to review the product specifications agreed upon?

- **DON'T GIVE YOUR POWER AWAY.**

    It's common in meetings to defer to a boss, others higher up in the organization, or someone who intimidates you. However, you may be giving away your power in the process. Learn to leverage these great opportunities, and use them instead to shine, by sharing who you are and revealing yourself as an influential player in the organization. Senior executives will take notice when someone—especially a so-called underling—stands firm with his or her own ideas. Look for opportunities to showcase your strengths and competencies. Champion yourself by acknowledging that what you bring to the table is as valid as anyone else's contributions.

- **REALIZE THAT YOUR CONTRARY THOUGHTS ARE WORTH SHARING, TOO.**

    When another meeting attendee shares a view contrary to yours, don't automatically assume that you are wrong and the other person is right. You may assign someone else's ideas greater importance than your own because you don't believe that your thoughts are worth sharing. That's simply not true. Not only are your experiences and opinions valid and worthwhile, but they also may be exactly what other people need to hear.

- **LEVERAGE YOUR EXPERTISE AND KNOWLEDGE CAPITAL.**

    Remind yourself how much you know, and of your talents and expertise. Recalling your knowledge helps you deliver this information confidently.

- **BE AN EFFECTIVE, CLEAR, AND ARTICULATE COMMUNICATOR.**

    As former Toastmasters International president Jana Barnhill says, "Being an effective communicator sets you apart from others. . . . When you are in a meeting, several of you may have the same thoughts. By being the one who can most clearly articulate your knowledge [and] your thoughts, you will be noticed."[7]

- **BE THE FIRST TO SPEAK UP.**

  Look for opportunities in each meeting to make your presence known early on. Try to speak up within the first 10 minutes, or be the first to express your viewpoint. The sooner you contribute, the less time you have to generate self-doubt by comparing others' statements to your own opinion. When you delay speaking up, you become withdrawn and find it harder to break into the discussion. So lead the discussion instead of following it, and reap the benefits of being fully engaged in every meeting.

- **STOP BEING PERFECT.**

  We often feel so much pressure to say what is right that we don't say anything at all. Lower your expectations and be okay with whatever you say. This will help you feel free to actually *speak*. Take quick action and make a statement before you stop yourself. Don't let perfectionism get in the way of your expression.

- **SPEAK UP ABOUT WHAT OTHERS ARE SAYING.**

  Add to what others are saying by affirming and endorsing their thoughts. This is an effective way to have your voice heard and for you to become comfortable with speaking during meetings. Mary Tung, a director at Lockheed Martin, "learned that if she couldn't add to the conversation during a meeting, she would take notes and keep track of all the main points being discussed. 'Then, at the end, I would interject and say, "Can I recap? Can I summarize?" You would be surprised how many people don't have that consolidated list. All of a sudden you have just added significant value to that meeting.' "[8]

- **PROPOSE SOLUTIONS.**

  Be proactive in suggesting solutions to problems or issues that arise. Even if you don't want the extra responsibility that might come from the suggested solution, take the initiative anyway. This will help others see you as a knowledgeable expert who can provide value.

How to Disagree at Meetings in a Positive and Productive Way

No one relishes an uncomfortable conversation, but sidestepping tough discussions can leave important issues unaddressed, creating even bigger problems.

—Adele B. Lynn
Author and consultant

A high-level executive at Levi Strauss & Company hired me for executive coaching. He wanted to know how he could articulate disagreement during meetings in a positive and productive fashion. Since he tended to be quiet and not speak up when he didn't agree with something, his silence was sometimes perceived as agreement when he in fact *didn't* agree.

This executive had no problem disagreeing with his manager. However, he worried that his contrary opinion would make him seem disagreeable when he was speaking with someone whom he didn't know very well, especially when the person was senior to him. I asked him, "So, what would happen if you aren't agreeable? Do you think it would hinder your job? Do you believe that not being agreeable makes others not like you or want to help when you need it?" I've *never* seen that happen to any client. Many clients who have similar challenges speaking up tend to want to have all the data and facts together before agreeing with or opposing someone. The benefit of collecting the facts before speaking is that you will be prepared and sound competent. The downside, however, is that you end up missing the chance to actively participate in the conversation. While you are waiting for the facts, you end up not sharing.

The Levi Strauss client implemented the suggestions that are outlined for you in this section and immediately reaped positive results. He noticed that it was easier for him to disagree during meetings. He also received more respect from others because he didn't stay silent or back down. Members of senior management told him how they appreciated his feedback, insights, and wisdom.

Sharing your opinions during meetings—even if they are contrary to what others might be saying—is necessary for others to see you as part of the conversation. As the discussion continues and others begin to participate, your opinion directly affects the flow and content. If you don't plan to speak, then why even attend the meeting? You are there to take part in a collaborative process that involves various individuals—yourself included—stating their points of view. People add to what others are saying, and ultimately reach a solution, direction, result, or action plan. Speaking allows you to become a part of that mix by adding to the conversation.

People become aware of your experience, knowledge capital, and expertise when you share at meetings. If you don't share, everyone misses out on that information. You're doing the meeting—and the entire organization—a disservice by refusing to contribute. Your coworkers lose out on hearing your opinions and becoming privy to your knowledge. They miss out on the suggestions and valuable information you could potentially share. Leaders want people who disagree. They want to be challenged with counter opinions.

Remember, you're not trying to sound entirely competent and proficient; you're adding your opinion to take part in the conversation and, ultimately, to help find a solution. Once you understand this, you'll be able to eliminate the need to first gather all the facts before speaking and you will fear rejection less.

Review the 16 tips presented in the previous section on increasing visibility at meetings. Many of them can be applied to meetings in which you might have disagreement. In addition, the following suggestions specifically cover how to disagree in a positive and productive manner.

- **SHARE YOUR KNOWLEDGE SO OTHERS BENEFIT.**

    Speak up to share your knowledge and expertise, and don't let the fears of disagreement stop you. Make yourself a part of the conversation. People want to hear what you have to say.

- **MIRROR THE PERSON WHO IS DISAGREEING.**

    When the person who disagrees speaks, make sure to respond by repeating what he or she has said word for word. For example, "Correct me if I'm wrong, but what you are saying is . . ." This helps people feel as though others have heard and understood them. Once they're under the impression that others are listening to and understanding them, they are then able to listen more carefully to what you have to say.

- **VALIDATE THE PERSON WHO IS DISAGREEING.**

    As you respond with a conflicting opinion, first explain to the person that you understand what he or she is saying with a phrase such as "It makes sense to me that . . ." Your ability to acknowledge and validate divergent opinions has more than one benefit. It helps you understand more fully the point of view that is different from your own. And it lowers people's defenses so that they are open to what you have to say.

- **BE PREPARED FOR CONTRARY VIEWPOINTS.**

    Before attending a meeting in which disagreement might occur, imagine some potential reasons why others might question your point of view. Then come up with sound and logical arguments to counter these viewpoints.

- **KNOW WHY YOUR IDEAS MUST BE HEARD.**

    Realize that you're an important part of the company and that you have expertise and experience that other people value. When you share, you elevate the conversation to another level. Don't do the company or yourself a disservice by keeping your opinions to yourself.

Summary and Action Steps

Before moving on to Chapter 7, where you'll be learning how initiative impacts visibility as well as 38 ways to gain visibility, here are the Chapter 6 summary and action steps.

Summary

- *The personality that shows up in your relationship with visibility is different for each person.* You've determined which personality—observer, participant, initiator, or leader—represents you. Depending on the situation in which you find yourself (with family, friends, colleagues, subordinates, senior executives, or others), you may exhibit different personalities.
- *Speak up, speak first, and speak often.* The Anderson and Kilduff study has proven that you'll be perceived as competent when you speak first and often, even when you don't actually possess that level of competence. Don't let fear of failure or others' judgments stop you from speaking up.
- *Meetings are an excellent place to gain visibility.* People get to know you and value your expertise and knowledge when you speak up at meetings. Don't wait until your comment is perfect and therefore risk losing the chance to speak up; instead, give yourself permission to participate as soon as possible.
- *Share your difference of opinion at meetings.* Meetings during which disagreement occurs are opportunities to make your opinion known in the conversation. This helps to move the conversation forward toward a possible agreement.

Take Action Now

- With which of the four personality types (observer, partici-pant, initiator, leader) do you identify most closely? As we've stated previously, different circumstances can bring out different personality types. Observe yourself through-out the week, and notice which of the four shows up with your family, friends, peers at work, boss, subordinates, sen-ior management, and others.

- Identify two different situations in which you decide to speak up and speak often. You might have to leave your comfort zone, but do it. You'll be heard and seen as compe-tent, and you'll notice others' perceptions of you starting to shift favorably as you contribute more often.

- Look at your calendar and choose the meetings during which you will participate. Push yourself out of your com-fort zone and speak up more than you are used to. What kind of response do you receive? Do people treat you differently?

- Review the list on "How to Be Visible at Meetings." Type up this list and take it to your meetings to serve as a re-minder. Choose different points to focus on until you've experimented with all 16.

- If you have one meeting in which disagreement commonly occurs and you are afraid to speak up, choose to do so—and don't wait until you have all the facts or have honed the perfect statement. Speak up without preparing in advance; you'll be a part of the collaborative process instead of sit-ting on the sidelines. Review the five suggestions that will help you disagree in a positive manner.

7

Raise Your Profile

It is important for aspiring managers to make themselves visible to those with higher authority in order to increase their prospects for promotion.

—Bernard M. Bass
Author and professor emeritus, State University of New York

Take the Initiative to Be Visible

A survey was conducted in which executives were asked, "What do you feel is the single best way for employees to earn a promotion and/or raise?" Topping the list for 82 percent of respondents was "ask for more work and responsibility."[1] The advice couldn't be any clearer: *If you want to gain a promotion, take the initiative and request an increase in responsibility.*

Being visible requires one important trait: initiative. In the book *1001 Ways to Take Initiative at Work*, author Bob Nelson explains, "By taking initiative, *all* employees can elevate their visibility within an organization and greatly improve their chances for recognition, learning, growth, pay raises, bonuses, and advancement for good performance."[2]

However, most people resist taking on an increase in responsibility because they don't want the added burden that's associated with more work. This failure to volunteer for more projects and tasks directly affects their professional visibility. As the *Harvard Business Review on Leadership* states, "Getting people to assume greater responsibility is not easy. Not only are many lower-level employees comfortable being told what to do, but many managers are accustomed to treating subordinates like machinery requiring control."[3]

What Is Initiative?

Initiative is doing the right things without being told.
—Elbert Hubbard
American writer, publisher, artist, and philosopher

Initiative means taking action without being asked. It's being able to see that something needs to be done and doing it, even if it's not within one's usual realm of responsibility. *Good to Great* author Jim Collins highlights the importance of taking responsibility when he explains, "The right people understand that they do not have 'jobs'—they have responsibilities. They grasp the difference between their task list and their true responsibilities. The right people can complete the statement, 'I am the one person ultimately responsible for . . . '"[4]

It's no coincidence that companies that have a reputation for producing great managers are those that foster a sense of leadership throughout their ranks. In fact, according to a survey by global management firm the Hay Group, 90 percent of these companies *expect* employees to lead, regardless of whether they have a formal position of authority.[5]

Leaders at all levels see opportunities where others do not. This occurs when you take an action that produces a result when it wasn't necessarily your job to take that action. It takes place when you don't wait for permission or instructions before jumping in. Initiative means that you notice what isn't working, create a solution for the problem, gain buy-in from your boss, and implement the desired outcome. Without initiative, attaining visibility is nearly impossible. Walter Shipley, former CEO of Chase Manhattan, says, "The people who are going to stand out are those who take the initiative and are self-motivated to anticipate what the next need is."[6]

Starbucks stores provide two great examples of initiative. First is the story of a Los Angeles Starbucks store manager who purchased her own blender to create a drink she invented because company CEO Howard Schultz didn't want to invest in blenders. For that reason, this particular store manager took the initiative, created the product in her own store, and tested it with her customers. As more and more people requested the product, Schultz ultimately ended up being convinced to invest in blenders for the drink. Since then, the Frappuccino has brought hundreds of millions of dollars to Starbucks.[7]

The second story comes from a Starbucks store manager who had a passion for music and began playing a variety of different types of music he liked at his stores. Customers kept asking to buy the music, but it wasn't for sale. So this manager approached Starbucks executives and asked, "Why not compile our own CD or tape? Customers would snap it up." The head honchos at Starbucks listened to this manager, and now CDs are sold in almost every one of the coffee shop's locations.[8]

At UPS, managers regularly share stories about employees that reinforce the behaviors they want to see more. These stories help UPS employees take the initiative and do more than what is expected. An example is "the driver who was delivering a package on Christmas Eve to a military base in Aberdeen,

> *The people who are going to stand out are those who take the initiative and are self-motivated to anticipate what the next need is.*
> —Walter Shipley

Maryland. The address wasn't properly filled out, but instead of leaving the package at the base to be routed later, the driver made the extra effort to locate the soldier, who was grateful because it contained a surprise gift—airline tickets for a flight later that day that would allow him to be home for Christmas."[9]

Why Are You Afraid of Initiative?

[D]on't be timid. Load the ship and set out. No one knows for certain whether the vessel will sink or reach the harbor. Just don't be one of those merchants who won't risk the ocean!

—Rumi
Thirteenth-century poet, theologian, and mystic

People don't take the necessary initiative needed for visibility because they become used to the limits of their current commitments and responsibilities. They are comfortable where they are and remain within these self-imposed boundaries. Passivity and too much patience begin to hinder their success. The authors of a recent *Harvard Business Review* article point out that "patience can be a curse for emerging leaders. It can undermine our potential by persuading us to keep our heads down and soldier on, waiting for someone to recognize our efforts and give us the proverbial tap on the shoulder—a better title and formal authority."[10] This tendency causes employees to do everything by the book, and nothing out of the ordinary. They start acting like a politician running for election—one who doesn't define his platform or agenda, who doesn't say anything that could be viewed negatively, and who says only what the voters want to hear.

This is precisely why constantly taking the initiative will allow you to stand out radically from others. You'll be different

from the individuals who keep
doing just enough to get by.
People who don't take the initiative feel as though their company will take care of them
without their needing to do
anything extra. They just keep

> *One measure of a leader's
> effectiveness is the number of
> initiatives he or she personally
> champions.*
> —John Zenger and Joseph
> Folkman

doing what is asked of them and figure that if they do
that competently, everything else will be fine. But the harsh
reality is that this assumption simply isn't true—especially in a
depressed economic climate. Once you understand the need to
go above and beyond just getting by, you'll be motivated to take
the necessary initiative.

Key Questions to Ask Yourself

Action is my domain. It's not what I say but what I do that matters.
—Gandhi
Indian human rights activist and spiritual leader

In the book *The Extraordinary Leader*, authors John Zenger
and Joseph Folkman express the importance of owning as many
initiatives as possible when they explain:

One measure of a leader's effectiveness is the number of initiatives he or she personally champions. What projects has this
leader started? What outcomes have this leader's fingerprints all
over them? What has happened that would not have occurred had
this leader not been present? The leader with initiative stops to
consider the current reality and asks questions such as:

- What is missing that would make a big difference?
- What needs to be done that only I can do?
- What [one task] could I do that would make a significant
  difference to the performance of this work team?
- What are others expecting me to do?[11]

In the 1990s, a female executive named Dawn Lepore was promoted to the position of chief information officer (CIO) at Charles Schwab. At this time, there were only a few women in charge of technology at major corporations. The board was therefore shocked that she was promoted, and several members reacted by questioning why it was done. Some even stated, "That was a really dumb decision, putting a woman in charge of technology." But as Lepore explains, "The reason I got the job was that I took on really tough assignments, things nobody wanted, things that people thought were kind of impossible or thankless tasks. So I proved that I could take on things I didn't know, and learn. I was willing to take risks, and I've always been a good synthesizer. And I was good at building relationships across the company."[12]

A client of mine at Oracle who wanted to improve her visibility with top management took a similar approach. She recognized that her vice president (who was three levels above her) had two sales initiatives that were extremely important to him. She also realized that no one in her department was focusing on these initiatives, thereby causing the VP to become increasingly frustrated by the lack of progress. My client saw this as an opportunity and chose to make one of the initiatives her own. She got approval from her immediate boss to proceed, and then met with her boss's boss and his peers on a regular basis to create support for her ownership of this initiative. My client used this opportunity to build visibility with members of senior leadership to whom she would not have otherwise been exposed.

By jumping in completely, owning and leading the sales initiative, my client ensured that the VP would automatically perceive her as the leader she now is. She gained the visibility, influence, and respect she desired.

Creating visibility comes from taking the initiative. What may seem impossible to others may be the very task that gives you the visibility you need. If you implement the many ideas suggested throughout this section on initiative, your professional circumstances will substantially shift. You'll get noticed, advance quickly, and gain the competitive advantage necessary to be an in-demand leader.

Seven Ways to Gain Visibility and Raise Your Profile

A "known" employee has the advantage over one who is not known.
—Susan M. Heathfield
American management and organizational development specialist

There are countless ways for you to become visible right now, to stand out and get noticed, and to have others recognize you. Don't wait for your comfort level to improve or until your next promotion. Don't wait for your boss to give you permission. Don't even wait to finish this book. Start *right now!* I will make it as easy as possible, by providing you with 38 suggestions in seven categories on gaining visibility and raising your profile. Before looking at the detailed tips, skim over the seven ways to gain visibility (see Figure 7.1). Go with your immediate gut reaction and circle the top three areas that you need to be doing to gain more visibility. Pay more attention to these three categories as you review the suggestions.

1. Seek out projects.
2. Leverage your manager.
3. Gain face time with top executives.
4. Find cross-departmental opportunities.
5. Become involved outside your job.
6. Speak up and share.
7. Become known and recognized.

1. Seek Out Projects

- *Be on high-profile projects.* Involve yourself in high-profile projects so that your name comes up frequently (and

FIGURE 7.1 Seven Ways to Gain Visibility

positively) in discussions at the top levels of the company. Taking part in projects that others consider to be a success can do wonders for enhancing the way you're perceived inside the company.

- *Take on the riskier projects.* When you take on a project that is deemed risky or one that other people avoid, and you manage and complete it successfully, others will begin to see you as someone who can achieve the impossible.
- *Ask for more responsibility.* Increased responsibility both aids your managers and/or colleagues and helps you gain visibility opportunities, as enhanced responsibility brings augmented exposure.
- *Get assigned to new projects.* Be willing to take on new projects or pilot new ideas. This involves taking risks because

the projects could fail. However, it also provides an opportunity to prove that something can work—thus gaining recognition for yourself.

- *Take on projects that nobody wants.* Though they might be undesirable, these projects might be deemed important. Take the advice of Walt Bettinger, president and CEO of Charles Schwab: "Go to your boss and say, 'Give me the dirtiest, nastiest, toughest problem you've got on your plate that has not been solved and let me have a crack at it.'"[13] Choose projects that directly affect business results, but that may not have easy solutions. You'll have a chance to gain incredible visibility if the project is successful; and even if it fails, you will be seen as someone who is willing to try.

- *Become involved in the hottest projects.* Identify the most up-to-date and influential projects, as well as the business unit working on them. These are the projects deemed trendy right now—the ones toward which the company is putting the majority of resources, time, money, and energy. The trend might last for months or years, so you want to be on this train. It has all the potential for you to gain recognition.

- *Make sure to add value to projects.* Look for opportunities to exceed expectations on the project you are currently working on. This is not about just doing your job well; it requires doing additional work. The value you've added to the project becomes known by others. This increases your visibility and puts you in contact with influential people.

2. Leverage Your Manager

- *Suggest to your manager ways that you can contribute more.* Identify areas in which you could contribute that would directly increase others' awareness of you. Share your suggestions with your manager and have your manager support the related implementation.

- *Create opportunities to represent your business unit.* Have your boss support your involvement in running or participating in the many meetings he or she attends. This creates great visibility for you and also helps your boss by freeing up his or her time, because your boss no longer needs to attend some of these meetings.

- *Share your accomplishments during your weekly one-on-one.* Share with your boss stories about what happened during the week that show how you've contributed to projects and people interactions. Your manager needs to hear about your wins to understand how much value you bring to the organization. I suggest keeping track of your wins throughout your week by documenting them on a daily basis. If you wait until the morning of your one-on-one, you'll forget many of your powerful achievements.

- *Have your boss inform his or her boss of your value.* Your boss's boss needs to know the kind of work you are doing. For this to happen, your boss must actively share all the important areas you are working on, the successes you are having, and the overall impact you have had on the department. Discuss with your boss why it's important to increase your visibility and exposure to his or her boss. It will take more work off of your boss's plate and expand your leadership responsibilities.

- *Have clients, customers, or vendors sing your praises.* These groups can share compliments about you via e-mail or voice mail. Whenever you do something positive above and beyond expectations, solve problems, or provide top-notch service, make sure to ask the person you're serving to tell your superiors (your boss and boss's boss) about it.

3. Gain Face Time with Top Executives

- *Identify and obtain exposure to key decision makers in your company.* Make a list of all the key decision makers in your organization, and create a strategy to become visible to each of them. You might need an introduction from another colleague to contact these individuals for advice, support, or mentorship.

- *Gain face time with the C-level executives.* Don't be intimidated by a person's title, reputation, or fame. After all, they were all where you are today at one time in their careers! Reach out to them and make sure they know who you are. They will genuinely appreciate the initiative.

- *Create time with the most influential people in your organization.* Find the executives with influence in the company and attend the meetings, conference calls, and interactions they attend. The more face time you have with executives, the better the chance that they will know you and see your worth to the company.

- *Seek out the answer when a higher-level leader asks a question.* When a higher-up lacks clarity on a situation or is pondering something new and isn't able to get the answer he or she needs in that moment, seek out the answer and provide it.

- *Have mentors introduce you to top executives.* Make sure that you have a few mentors who have networks of executives with whom they interact regularly. As your mentors get to know you and your work, they'll come to see that connecting you with these influential individuals will benefit everyone.

- *Associate with the top executives who have the best reputations.* The executive with the established reputation and solid credibility is the one with whom you want to associate, since this will compel other leaders to see you positively.

4. Find Cross-Departmental Opportunities

- *Find projects outside your own line of business.* Identify tasks that will gain you exposure to other business units besides your own, and that will allow you to interact with leaders and peers who don't know you. They will understand the value you produce and seek you out in the future for your knowledge and expertise.

- *Look for opportunities to be on cross-functional teams.* Identify specific projects or assignments that will pair you with teams besides your own. This is an excellent way to have other leaders in the company notice your value-adding work.

- *Mentor people in other departments.* As you mentor people, you will become visible to the leaders of other departments. This will reflect back on you positively when your mentee gains more success. Your mentee will also praise you to other members of his or her department.

- *Include the human resources (HR) department in your accomplishment updates.* Make your company's human resources professionals an asset in your career. Keep them involved in your contributions and overall impact on the company. They are often a forgotten department that actually has some pull and influence. E-mail them an update that highlights your accomplishments once every four to six months. As one client said to me, "HR plays God with your career." Even though they aren't directly in control of your professional future, their opinions do have weight and they are often present for and influential in important career discussions.

5. Become Involved Outside Your Job

- *Attend internal training seminars.* Choose seminars based on the type of people who may attend. If people of influence attend sessions, this becomes an excellent way to meet them and make a strong impression in a low-key environment. You can gain visibility at these seminars by speaking up in what is usually a more comfortable situation.

- *Become involved in professional/trade associations.* Be active and involved in one or two professional/trade associations, and take a leadership role to increase your visibility. Make sure that the position you undertake is aligned to your industry so that it will be announced companywide. This creates a great amount of company public promotion about you.

- *Attend industry-related conferences.* You can either speak at or just attend these conferences. As a speaker, you provide your company with good visibility, which reflects well on you. As an attendee, you gain knowledge that enhances your expertise, which you can then share with your colleagues on your return.

- *Be a part of your company's internal programs (for example, mentoring).* Whether it's a brown-bag lunch workshop or a formal mentoring program, it's important to be involved in activities that will introduce you to people beyond your business unit.

- *Become involved in special committees.* Beyond your normal day-to-day job, identify any internal committees or task forces in your company that have projects and leadership roles with which you can become involved. These committees help you gain exposure across the company to people who are in different offices and at various levels.

- *Participate in your company's volunteer opportunities.* Volunteer time to projects that give you an opportunity to meet higher-level leaders outside of your formal work environment. You'll share common ground on nonwork subjects and build a rapport that connects the two of you.

- *Attend holiday parties and outside company events.* These environments make it easier for you to introduce yourself to people you don't know but need to know. The art of small talk can help you make a strong and lasting impression.

- *Contribute to a publication.* You create immediate visibility and quickly become known as an expert when you use your knowledge to write for publications. You can choose to write for outside sources or internal newsletters and blogs.

- *Teach a training class locally or nationally.* Find a training class to teach that will help you become recognized as an expert in a certain area and will increase your exposure throughout the company.

6. Speak Up and Share

- *Share your ideas and solutions.* Companies are desperate for ideas and ways to generate new revenue, improve customer service, streamline operations, and reduce expenses. Actively seek out opportunities to present your ideas so that others will appreciate what you know and the work you have done. The attention that your big ideas generate will provide increased visibility.

- *Offer suggestions.* When appropriate, offer to management suggestions that might help the organization improve product quality or employee morale. Ideas to help with financial stability and customer service can also be helpful. Offering innovative, workable ideas can earn you a reputation as someone who makes a difference. Always be ready to take ownership and responsibility for your suggestions.

- *Make presentations.* When you present, you are *being* visible. Others come to know you and hear your ideas. Use this opportunity to make a great impression on many. They will see what you do and how well you do it.

7. Become Known and Recognized

- *Make yourself memorable.* People with power and influence need to remember you. What, specifically, is memorable about the work you do? What do you do that is unique and makes you stand out from the rest? Whatever it is, make sure this is what people know and remember about you.

- *Build name recognition.* Your name needs to be known. You are your own brand—so the more people out there who know your name, the better. Make sure your name is included on all major projects and assignments you undertake and complete. Write a story or provide a quote for your industry association publication or your company's newsletter that details your involvement in the process.

- *Become an expert in your industry.* As you become recognized as an expert, people will seek you out for your knowledge and consider you to be an industry leader. Find speaking opportunities that highlight your expertise at conferences and trade shows.

- *Act above yourself.* If you want to land a better position, do what you can now to act as if you are already performing at that level. For example, if you want to become a director, act like a director even though you hold a position below that level.

Summary and Action Steps

Before moving on to Part Three, which focuses on influence, here are the Chapter 7 summary and action steps:

Summary

- *Initiative is necessary for visibility to occur.* The more initiative you take at work, the more visibility you gain and impact you make.

- *Initiative is taking on opportunities where others don't see them.* Don't wait to jump in and solve a problem; when something isn't working, fix it.
- *Don't let complacency stop you from taking the initiative.* People prefer not to take the initiative because they get comfortable with their current roles and responsibilities. The one competitive advantage that helps you stand out from others is the ability to take the initiative.
- *Become visible right now.* Don't wait to feel comfortable. Many suggestions, ideas, and tips on ways to gain visibility and raise your profile are available for you to take action on and thereby become highly visible. You can seek out projects, leverage your manager, gain face time with top executives, find cross-departmental opportunities, become involved outside your job, speak up and share, and become known and recognized.

Take Action Now

- Take the initiative by asking your boss and/or boss's boss for more responsibility. Show them you are capable of handling more without undermining your current job duties.
- Review the questions outlined in the section titled "Key Questions to Ask Yourself," and jot down your answers to each. Create a plan to take the initiative based on your responses.
- Review the "Seven Ways to Gain Visibility and Raise Your Profile." Decide which category is most relevant at this stage in your career. Select at least two ideas from within this category and implement them over the next month.
- If all seven categories are important, select one category per week and employ all those action steps for the entire week. Do this for seven weeks and you'll see the dramatic benefits of becoming visible.

Part Two—Visibility Conclusion

You now understand the importance that visibility plays in getting noticed, recognized, and promoted. The value of speaking up and becoming known is a vital piece of your career management. Leveraging the three-step promotion plan—self-promote, promote others, have others promote you—will provide a solid foundation for launching your visibility. By implementing the tips and suggestions provided throughout the visibility section, you will increase your exposure across the entire organization and become known as a valued leader.

Bonus Online Material

How visible are you at work? Do you stand out and get noticed by the people who matter most? Take the free assessment at www.GarfinkleExecutiveCoaching.com/assessments-visibility.html to find out. Through this evaluation, you'll learn the top 10 areas you must emphasize to increase your visibility.

Perception + Visibility = Influence

Now you are ready for the book's third and final section on influence. The two pillars that support influence are perception and visibility; influence can't happen unless you have improved your perception and increased your visibility. Once you've established the appropriate level of perception, you'll have gained a solid reputation and foundation of respect. Once you have increased your visibility, you'll become known and valued in your company. Influence is now possible.

With influence comes impact, which is ultimately what makes influence so different from perception and visibility. Your ability to have impact when working on the areas of perception and visibility is limited; however, you enjoy unrestricted impact when you begin to work on your influence. Influence is an empty vessel of unlimited potential to change and alter situations—as Part Three shows.

Part Three

Exert Your Influence—Lead Situations,
People, and Events

8

Lead through Influence

All leadership is influence.

—John C. Maxwell
American author, speaker, and pastor

Relentlessly Chase Perfection

Vince Lombardi came to the Green Bay Packers in 1959 for his first head coaching opportunity. Though he had been an assistant in college and pro football, he had no experience as a head coach. In fact, Lombardi was known by so few people that a prominent member of the Packers' board, when told who had become the head coach, responded by asking, "Vince who?"

And make no mistake, this National Football League (NFL) franchise was indeed in a position where it could have used a well-known, highly regarded leader. Coach Lombardi was taking over a team that, after 12 straight losing seasons, had just had its worst season ever—one during which it won only one game out of the 12 played. The Packers were in fact *so* bad that they almost lost their franchise completely.

Though largely unheard of, Coach Lombardi was a leader who recognized the importance of influence. He knew he needed to establish influence early on and make his determination for winning known. At the time, this game-losing team had no respect; it had become known as the laughingstock of the entire NFL. From the very beginning of his tenure as coach, however, Lombardi set the right tone. He said, "I have never been on a losing team, gentlemen, and I do not intend to start now."

One of the first points Lombardi ever made to the entire Green Bay team was: "Gentlemen, we are going to relentlessly chase perfection, knowing full well we will not catch it, because nothing is perfect. But we are going to relentlessly chase it, because in the process we will catch excellence."[1] Bart Starr, the Hall of Fame quarterback for the majority of games that Lombardi coached at Green Bay, remembers Lombardi "walking right up to [the team], within a foot of us in the front row, and then [saying], 'I am not remotely interested in just being good.'" This team went on to win five NFL Championships, won Super Bowls I and II, and never had a losing season.

Just as Coach Lombardi was able to overcome his own obscurity to turn a downtrodden franchise into one of the best football teams of all time, you, too, can transform your role and initiate your impact. You can set the right tone, establish commitment, create buy-in, and influence change. *An organization's true leaders are the individuals who leverage their influence to make change.* The key is being committed to excellence. Vince Lombardi didn't stand for just being good—and neither should you. The next level in your success is possible, but you must be willing to take the leap, assume the risks, and have courage. You must be ready to make your impact known by being the influential person you are capable of being.

Coach Lombardi knew the benefits that come from leading through influence. Despite the fact that he started from nothing, he was able to achieve greatness. The lasting and important changes he made came from using the power of influence on a daily basis.

What Is Influence?

Who shall set a limit to the influence of a human being?
—Ralph Waldo Emerson
American essayist, lecturer, and poet

So what exactly *is* influence? Influence occurs when you have the power to alter or change a situation. It could mean swaying just one other person or a large group, undertaking a major project, or creating new initiatives. In short, you influence the outcome of something by improving it, and you make important decisions that have impact. Influential people do what others deem to be important. Warren Bennis, University Professor and Distinguished Professor of Business Administration at the University of Southern California, explains, "The basis of leadership is the capacity of the leader to change the mind-set [and] the framework of another person."

Ask yourself these questions to see how influential you currently are:

- Has someone above you in the chain of command recently acted on one of your ideas and given you credit?
- Do your employees act on your requests and delegations swiftly and accurately?
- Do your peers get on board with your cross-organization initiatives?
- Do people buy into your projects and ideas?
- Do you constantly take the initiative in leading projects and assignments?

> *People with influence make things happen.*

People with influence make things happen. They move their organizations forward by taking action and producing powerful results. They use their visibility to extend their influence and make an impact. These people inspire others to execute and accomplish a significant amount, irrespective of power or authority. They make the tough and important decisions. Famed business leader Jack Welch discusses the value of making the difficult decisions. He says, "A lot of people have good ideas, and good values, and they can even energize others. But for some reason they are not able to make the tough calls. That is what separates . . . whether or not someone can lead a business."[2]

To truly have influence is to cultivate power in places where you *don't* have authority. Influence then becomes about voluntary engagement. In the *Handbook of Leadership Theory and Practice*, authors Nitin Nohria and Rakesh Khurana say that the essence of leadership is "to get people voluntarily to do things that they would not otherwise do."[3] You are able to sway opinions and have people embrace your ideas and perspectives. They go along with what you want, and are loyal to your ideas. You motivate and arouse interest in others to do what is deemed important. Influence means gaining others' support to move situations and projects forward. As Roy Johnson and John Eaton say in their book, *Influencing People*, "When you succeed in getting your ideas heard and accepted, you are exerting influence."[4]

People who already have authority must use influence instead of relying solely on power to accomplish what they want. Depending too much on your established authority can minimize your ability to gain commitment and change from the people you're trying to influence. While one group or individual might respect that positional power and follow your lead, others will not. Therefore, you need to use the influence that comes from an authentic and trusted place of authority—one that has nothing to do with your position in the company.

An established reputation, high degree of respect, valued expertise, and deep knowledge help create a strong foundation

> *To truly have influence is to cultivate power in places where you don't have authority.*

of influence. In her *Harvard Business Review* article, author Linda A. Hill reinforces the point about not relying too much on authority by explaining that "we see a new manager fall into the trap of relying too heavily on his formal authority as his source of influence. Instead, he needs to build his influence by creating a web of strong, interdependent relationships, based on credibility and trust, throughout his team and the entire organization—one strand at a time."[5]

How Influence Affects Three Stages of Your Career

Depending on where you are in your career, you will need and apply influence differently. The use of influence by an individual contributor is minimal, but important to understand. Managers recognize that influence is necessary for future success, and use it to help establish their value in the company. Leaders use and leverage influence the most.

Let's look at how each of these three career stages relates to the level of influence you must develop and exert.

Individual Contributor

Despite the fact that one uses influence more frequently as a manager or leader, it's important to discuss how influence affects the individual contributor. You may be an individual contributor or may be managing people who are at this stage.

As an individual contributor, you mostly are at the mercy of others' influence. Everything around you influences you;

you enter your organization knowing little about it. You don't fully understand how everything works; you are overwhelmed by the amount of information coming at you; and you don't yet know what the rules of success are. When you're managing employees at the beginning of their careers, you should be aware that they probably feel like a deer in the headlights. Think of them as rookie quarterbacks; the ball is snapped and they're face-to-face with five 300-pound linemen aggressively ready to attack with all of their force. As the quarterback, you have only a couple of seconds to think fast, process what the defense is doing, make the right decision, and throw the ball.

Toward the end of your time as an individual contributor, you begin to establish a track record. Of course, this takes time, but you gain more confidence as you keep stacking up victories. Others begin to recognize your performance, which gives you the self-assurance and courage to look for opportunities for influence. While the majority of your influence will remain within your department, you are now beginning to understand its greater importance. Pay attention, and look to build key relationships at this point in your career. Stand out, get noticed, and let your talents shine.

Manager

As a manager, you begin to feel an established place in the work world. You understand your company's inner workings, how you are supposed to act, who the important players are, and how to prioritize your work. Your performance has continued to excel. You've begun to contribute a tremendous amount to the company. You're managing a team, and as such, you excel whenever your team members do.

Others are beginning to see you as a go-to person, a seasoned resource whom colleagues seek out for your advice and insights. As your value increases, so does your influence. At this established stage, influence is starting to occur. You are receiving promotions, raises, interesting projects, and enhanced responsibility. You are exhibiting your talents and value to the company. You've become known.

While this stage comes with many of the benefits just mentioned, it's also a period of time during which your career can plateau. This deceleration has a tendency to begin when you receive a title or position of authority. You might become comfortable with the false sense of power that your title grants you, and begin relying too much on your positional authority. This might cause you to forget how to influence without using the weight your position has given you. Unfortunately, positional authority can disappear or be taken from you in an instant; however, raw and authentic influence can never be taken away.

At this stage, people split into two groups. One group moves toward influence and continues advancing. Members of this group keep providing value, and can make the leap to the next level. The other group, however, becomes stuck in their careers. They don't know how to leverage influence for their own success and the company's, and so they remain where they are.

Leader

The next level has arrived. You've developed and honed the vital skills and talents necessary to be a leader. You're leading others, top management values you, and your peers have respect for you. You now have gone beyond establishing yourself; you have gained recognition. People appreciate your value, and need what you provide. They seek you out for your influence, and understand the full value of what you bring to situations. You've become an essential component in your company's success.

At this impact-making stage, you'll be influencing out-comes, contributing to major decisions, and driving change for the betterment of the company.

Why Influence Is Important

The good teacher discovers the natural gifts of his pupils and liber-ates them by the stimulating influence of the inspiration that he can impart. The true leader makes his followers twice the men they were before.

—Stephen Neill
Anglican missionary, bishop, and scholar

> *You can't be a leader unless you have influence. No one will follow you unless he or she believes in you.*

All leaders must manage through influence to be success-ful. Their abilities and strengths help them to accomplish what is deemed crucial, so that positive change can occur for the organization.

Leaders who use influence are excellent collaborators who bring people together to create solutions. They help everyone to become aligned so that the organization can achieve the desired results. They are able to bring successful coalitions together, and they know how to appeal to people's needs and turn them into advocates for their idea.

Influential leaders know how to build connections within their business units, cross-functionally, and with top manage-ment. As these relationships develop, influence begins to take hold and move things forward. As the relationship becomes more established and mutually respectful, those involved are able to exert greater influence. These leaders can mobilize peo-ple from different groups to create successful outcomes.

The number-one realization to keep in mind is this: You can't be a leader unless you have influence. No one will follow you unless he or she believes in you. People need to see that you're able to trigger change in people and projects.

Lead through Influence—Not Power, Authority, or Title

You don't have to hold a position in order to be a leader.
—Anthony J. D'Angelo

In the book *The Leader of the Future*, Charles Handy says, "A career is now not so much a ladder of roles, but a growing reputation for making things happen. Influence, not authority, is what drives . . . all organizations."[6] Many people make the false assumption that you need authority or power to have influence. This isn't true. Many people have managed to persuade others without any formal authority or title. In fact, it has been proven many times that influence without power has achieved some of the greatest accomplishments in history.

> *I have not the shadow of a doubt that any man or woman can achieve what I have, if he or she would make the same effort and cultivate the same hope and faith.*
> —Gandhi

For example, how could one man who was a mere five feet three inches tall, weighing only 100 pounds, and wearing only a dhoti and shawl take on an entire government and influence incredible change? This man had no power or authority; he only had his marches, boycotts, strikes, and nonviolent protests. Yet Mahatma Gandhi eventually wore down the British government to the point that they granted India independence from British rule.

Gandhi saw himself as a simple man who had great faith in his ability to enact change. He once said, "I claim to be no more than an average man with less than average abilities. I have not the shadow of a doubt that any man or woman can achieve what I have, if he or she would make the same effort and cultivate the same hope and faith."

Gandhi's influence stretches even further than the incredible advances he made in freeing his country from British rule. Just as a pebble is thrown into a lake and the ripples in the water have far-reaching impact, Gandhi prompted others to approach their own challenges in similar ways. He influenced Nelson Mandela to use this nonviolent method to overcome apartheid. Mandela had been stripped of all his power when he was sent to prison on an island and received the cruelest treatment imaginable by being isolated for months at a time and forced to stay in his cell 23 hours a day. Mandela proved for 27 years that he could be robbed of everything—except his influence. Even while in prison, he was able to make an impact that led to his release—and the eventual end of apartheid in South Africa. Similar to Gandhi, Mandela saw himself as a common man: "I was not a messiah, but an ordinary man who had become a leader because of extraordinary circumstances."[7]

Before Dr. Martin Luther King Jr. adopted Gandhi's nonviolent message, it was Rosa Parks who had the greatest influence on the entire Civil Rights movement, and especially on Dr. King himself. When this department store seamstress refused to give up her seat to a white man on a bus one evening in 1955, she ignited a bus boycott, one led by a young, not-yet-known 26-year-old Baptist minister named Dr. Martin Luther King Jr.

Parks's influence was so great that history has regarded her single act of defiance as the true beginning of the Civil Rights movement. Parks has said the following about her influential act: "People always say that I didn't give up my seat because I was tired, but that isn't true. I was not tired physically, or no more tired than I usually was at the end of a working day. I was not old, although some people have an image of me as being old then. I was forty-two. No, the only tired I was, was tired of

> *I was not a messiah, but an ordinary man who had become a leader because of extraordinary circumstances.*
> —Nelson Mandela

giving in. I knew someone had to take the first step and I made up my mind not to move. Our mistreatment was just not right, and I was tired of it."[8]

> *Power is not necessary. Authority is not necessary. A title is not necessary. What is necessary is influence.*

Power is not necessary. Authority is not necessary. A title is not necessary. What is necessary is *influence*—and the desire to be influential. No matter where you sit within the organization or in your life, you can make an impact. How else can you explain how a seamstress, a lawyer, and a minister went from being ordinary citizens to becoming extraordinary figures? They were just like you at one time, even though they went on to accomplish achievements that might seem like impossible feats.

You have more ability to influence situations than you realize. So don't wait to be influential; instead, start immediately. You have what it takes to be extraordinary. You can make an impact from where you are right now.

Evaluate Your Current Influence Ability

I refuse to accept the idea that man cannot influence the unfolding events that surround him.

—Martin Luther King Jr.
American clergyman and civil rights leader

What can you do to become a leader who influences others? Look at the 10 actions listed to see which ones you are currently doing, and which ones you need to develop. Though I've touched upon many of these points throughout the book, this list provides an organized way to digest and implement prior points in a way that's directly related to influence.

I encourage you to think, evaluate, question, and ponder each one of these points. They are simple and easy to relate to and comprehend. While achieving influence often seems a bit distant and too grand for some, everyone understands why each of these points is necessary and needed. Once you accomplish all 10, you reach a high level of influence.

Influence allows you to:

1. *Get things done.* People know they can count on you to accomplish even the toughest assignments.

2. *Become a go-to person.* Others seek you out for advice to accomplish the most essential tasks and to make important decisions.

3. *Build strong alliances.* You're able to create alliances across all business units, thereby developing a wider base of support and cooperation.

4. *Gain buy-in for your ideas.* Your established credibility and respect will prompt people to embrace your ideas and to want to be a part of what you are doing.

5. *Leverage your allies.* Your allies will help support your ideas and accomplish the tasks that have been deemed important.

6. *Sway decisions.* When you speak, people will listen to what you have to say so that you can sway decisions to your desired outcome.

7. *Cause others to rely on you.* When you influence decisions and change outcomes for the better, people appreciate your confidence and know they can depend on you.

8. *Lead up.* You'll establish mutual respect with people above you who want to seek out and hear your opinions, ideas, and insights.

9. *Gain results from others.* You will inspire others to take on activities that affect the organization and positively impact bottom-line results.

10. *Attract the star employees.* You'll create a committed, engaged, and excited workforce that executes the projects or activities related to what you are influencing.

Summary and Action Steps

Before moving on to Chapter 9, where you'll learn the five character traits that all people of influence have, here are the Chapter 8 summary and action steps.

Summary

- *People with influence make things happen.* They are the individuals who move companies forward and create powerful results.
- *Depending on where you are in your career, you will acquire and apply influence differently.* There are three different stages of your career—individual contributor, manager, and leader. You will use and leverage influence more frequently as you progress in your career.
- *You do not need authority or power to have influence.* Many people have influenced thousands of others without any formal title. No matter where you sit within an organization or in your life, you can make an impact.
- *You can become influential right now.* This chapter provides 10 quick ideas on how to become influential in order for you to take action and start moving your career in this direction.

Take Action Now

- Ask yourself the following questions: How influential are you? How do you use influence at work? Review the section "What Is Influence?" to help you generate ideas and information. Schedule 30 minutes this week to write out your answers.
- Figure out at which stage (individual contributor, manager, or leader) you are in your career. Look over the

section that directly applies to you and jot down two to three ideas that you can act on to improve your influence at your current stage.

• Write down five ways in which you have noticed others exerting influence *without* relying on their authority, power, or title. Observe your own behavior and come up with three action steps you can take that will allow you to do the same.

• Review the 10 ways to be influential highlighted at the end of the chapter and choose one to work on per week. Turn each suggestion into a question. For example, the second one—become a go-to person—would require you to ask, "What can I do to become the go-to person?" Implement the ideas you glean from each question.

9

Be Influential Now

The very essence of all power to influence lies in getting the other person to participate.

—Harry A. Overstreet
American social psychologist

How to Become Influential

There always are tangible steps you can take to enhance your ability to influence others. Although you may not yet believe in yourself, trust your own ability, or know how to wield influence, you should be assured that you *can*. Perhaps you don't have any role models, or haven't seen anyone who positively wields influence. Regardless of your current state of influence, the first step in increasing it is to be aware of the specific traits that influential people have developed to a significantly higher degree than others have.

Think of the three or four most influential people you know, and consider the traits they have in common. What makes them able to influence others? Your list should include many, if not all, of the following five areas (see Figure 9.1):

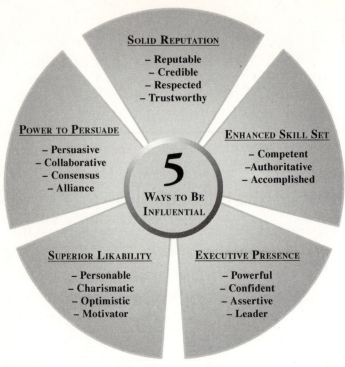

FIGURE 9.1   Five Ways to Be Influential

1. Solid reputation
2. Enhanced skill set
3. Executive presence
4. Superior likability
5. Power to persuade

Now, on a scale from 1 (poorly developed) to 10 (highly developed), grade yourself in each of these five areas. Mark your score next to each one listed. Don't be ashamed to score yourself a 1 or a 2. The point of this exercise isn't to wring your hands over your low grades, but to recognize that you have tremendous opportunity to grow in these five key areas.

High scores in each of these five characteristics *are* attainable, regardless of the stage you are at in your career—and each leads to greater influence. Simply begin working from wherever you are; you can start today. As long as you diligently implement these characteristics, you'll begin to notice a marked improvement.

Solid Reputation

The way to gain a reputation is to endeavor to be what you desire to appear.

—Socrates
Classical Greek Athenian philosopher

Your reputation is simply the way that others view you. When they interact with you, they experience who you are, what you do, your behaviors, and your personality. Other people's impressions form your reputation.

Reputations take time to build. Eventually, your accomplishments will begin proving your worth to the company. Due to your consistently helpful and effective behavior, others will start to view you as reliable and come to both know and respect you. They will find your character trustworthy and know that your actions will be consistent. They will value you and depend on you.

One advantage of a positive reputation is that when people meet you for the first time they will tend to think positively of you and give you the benefit of the doubt. They will have respect for you before you've even made your first real impression.

The challenge with a good reputation, however, is that it only takes one or two ways to ruin one that you've spent years building. Just look at the many celebrities, athletes, politicians, CEOs, and corporations that have ruined their good names with scandals, infidelities, fraud, money laundering, and other types of corruption. Benjamin Franklin said it well: "Glass, china, and reputation are easily cracked, and never mended well."

As you implement any of the following traits, you'll be building your solid reputation and making it a constant part of your current state.

Character Traits for a Solid Reputation

- *Reputable:* You have a solid reputation, good standing, and status. People count on you.
- *Credible:* You have accomplished goals that others value. When you speak, others listen.
- *Respected:* Others look up to and admire you. They want to be like you. You inspire others.
- *Trustworthy:* People depend on you, have complete faith in you, and see you as believable. They know you keep your promises and can be relied on.

Famous Examples of Solid Reputation **Peter Drucker**, the author of 40 business management books, gained a reputation as the most influential business strategist in the twentieth century and is credited for inventing the discipline of management. For over 50 years, he advised top corporations, well-known leaders, and executives. He predicted many of the monumental developments of the late twentieth century, including the critical importance of marketing and lifelong learning, as well as the emergence of Japan as an economic powerhouse.

Jane Addams, the first American woman to win the Nobel Prize for Peace, spent 50 years tirelessly working on behalf of women's suffrage, better working conditions of the urban poor, and world peace. The founder of modern social work, she started the first social settlement in the United States. At one point, she was deemed the most respected woman in the nation. Her credibility and stature led her to become the first woman ever to make a nominating speech at a national political convention. She nominated Theodore Roosevelt.

Questions for You to Consider ***What is your reputation?*** You'll begin to develop a greater understanding of the current state of your reputation as you answer the following questions: How do others view you? What reputation do you have with your peers, your subordinates, and the executives above you? Are you reliable? Do people feel that they can count on you? Are you consistent? Do you meet the expectations of others? Do you exceed them?

How can you improve your reputation? Can you be more of a team player? Can you enhance your involvement in each interaction you have with your colleagues? Can you be more dependable? Can you do more than others expect? Take initiative to solve problems that no one else wants to try to solve. Develop a status as someone who helps others and makes them better at what they do. Become a mentor. Increase your responsibility, and meet all expectations.

Enhanced Skill Set

> *If the next generation is to face the future with zest and self-confidence, we must educate them to be original as well as competent.*
> —Mihaly Csikszentmihalyi
> Hungarian psychology professor and author

Having an enhanced skill set is all about knowing how to do your job exceedingly well. People throughout the company recognize and know you as someone who is extremely competent. You have extensive knowledge capital. You do quality work and perform at the highest level. You maintain a level of excellence in all that you do. You constantly surprise people and exceed their expectations. This impresses others, which, in turn, increases the level of respect they have for you. And as respect increases, so does your influence.

Colleagues know you as someone whom others can count on. You are reliable. People feel they can trust you, and they know you'll get the job done. No matter how difficult or challenging situations become, you always do an excellent job. Others depend on your confidence and strength, and want you on their team. You are in demand and sought after. As your coworkers begin to lean on you for your enhanced skill set, your influence starts to take shape.

At this point, you leverage your competency and expertise in the execution of your work. You are a decisive decision maker and achieve results quickly. You come up with innovative solutions to challenging problems, and people take notice. They continue assigning you enhanced responsibility, and with each new level come new promotions and increased influence.

As you implement any of the following traits, you'll be building your enhanced skill set and making it a part of your current state.

Character Traits for an Enhanced Skill Set

- *Competent:* You are highly skilled and proficient at your job.
- *Authoritative:* You are an expert with clout who has valued knowledge in a certain area. People seek you out for your specific talents.
- *Accomplished:* You have a proven track record of achieving desired results.

Famous Examples of Enhanced Skill Sets   **Bill Gates**, founder of Microsoft Corporation, has a reputation as a brilliant technologist who cofounded one of the best-known and most successful companies—pretty impressive considering he was once referred to as shy and socially awkward. His enhanced skill set extends far beyond being a technological innovator, as he is also a strategic thinker and a philanthropist.

Jane Goodall, primatologist, humanitarian, and United Nations Messenger of Peace, has a reputation as the premier chimpanzee expert. She didn't hone these skills in a library or laboratory, but while working with chimps in the wilds of Africa, literally *living* with the very chimpanzees she studied. Her competence and authority on the subject eventually forced scientists to abandon their long-held definition of human beings as the only animals that use tools.

Questions for You to Consider   *How well do you apply the traits related to an enhanced skill set?* Do others see you as competent? Do you produce high-quality work? Do others leverage and utilize your knowledge? Do you have a reputation for not considering any project, problem, or issue too difficult to undertake or solve?

How can you improve your enhanced skill set? Identify projects or assignments that you can do to enhance your proven track record. Determine the desired results that your superiors regard as important and on which you can exceed expectations. Expand and develop a specific field of expertise so that others deem you an authority in this area. Choose to work on visible projects. When you complete them successfully, your reputation will improve, and you will be considered a highly competent person.

Executive Presence

> *The key is to keep company only with people who uplift you, whose presence calls forth your best.*
>
> —Epictetus
> Greek Stoic philosopher

Executive presence is about having a powerful and confident persona. The magnetic pull of your charismatic personality draws people to you and compels them to follow you. They trust in your leadership, and feed off of your assured sense of self.

You are a powerful force inside the organization. You don't hesitate; you take immediate action. You are decisive and confident with your choices, and you never waver. Even if you are wrong, it doesn't affect your outward demeanor. You simply try again. Taking risks is just a part of your natural approach.

You are assertive, and consistently move forward with what you want. When you believe in something, you put all your energy and force behind it. You are firm, but not forceful, with your ideas and opinions. The respect with which you treat others prevents them from viewing your assertiveness as aggressiveness. You create consensus with others so they feel included in the ideas that you encourage.

When you leverage your expertise and the areas in which you are competent, executive presence follows. You feel powerful about what you know. You are confident as your own strengths increase while others come to you for your knowledge capital.

As you develop the following traits, you'll build executive presence into a vital element of your current state.

Character Traits for Executive Presence
- *Powerful:* People perceive you as powerful.
- *Confident:* You are sure of yourself and certain in the decisions you make.
- *Assertive:* You take action confidently.
- *Leader:* People follow you with certainty, and you feel sure in guiding them.

Famous Examples of Executive Presence *Jack Welch*, former chairman and CEO of General Electric, gained a reputation as one of the world's top executives and business leaders. His self-assured nature provided a high level of confidence in all who followed him. He inspired his leaders to believe the impossible could be achievable. His no-nonsense, direct, and dynamic style helped turn GE into the most valued company in the world.

Eleanor Roosevelt, first lady of the United States and United Nations delegate, drafted the United Nations Declaration of Human Rights, and helped found UNICEF. In doing so, she earned a reputation as one of the most admired women in history, as well as being a prominent political figure who championed humanitarian efforts for civil rights, women's rights, children, and the poor. She redefined the role of first lady. Instead of standing in the shadow of her powerful husband, she became a passionate activist, held hundreds of press conferences, and wrote a daily column.

Questions for You to Consider *How much executive presence do you have?* Do others see you as confident? Does your personality draw people toward you? Are you decisive in making decisions? Do you assertively move your ideas forward?

What can you commit to do to improve your executive presence? Find specific ways in which you can show others that you make decisive and assertive choices. You want others to trust in your leadership, so emphasize your confidence in who you are, the choices you make, and your overall demeanor. Find an opinion or idea to share that shows that you don't waver. Reveal your knowledge and expertise so that others come to view you as competent and their respect for you grows.

In my book *Executive Presence* I detail the 16 characteristics necessary to develop executive presence. If you'd like to learn more, visit my website at www.GarfinkleExecutive Coaching.com.

Superior Likability

Charisma is a sparkle in people that money can't buy.
It's an invisible energy with visible effects.

—Marianne Williamson
American author on spiritual, personal, and political issues

Superior likability simply requires that other people like you and enjoy your company. Much as with executive presence, they are drawn to you. Your personality makes others feel comfortable, and you naturally put people at ease. They feel enriched and lifted up by your presence. They are excited to work for you, and want to help you in any way that you wish.

When you are likable, people go the extra mile for you. They protect you and will do whatever it takes to make sure you are successful. They want to help you, they care about you, and they are invested in you. When you want something done, they bend over backward to do an excellent job. Even people you don't know very well feel a kinship and closeness to you. They trust you quickly because of the comfort you provide in their presence. By establishing this kind of immediate trust, you create buy-in for your ideas.

All types of people from all levels of your organization like you. Whether it's the brand-new 22-year-old employee, the gruff 25-year company veteran down the hall, or the CEO, most people feel an inherent affinity toward you. Your ability to smoothly interact with a variety of different people is often leveraged to create coalition, especially in contentious situations.

As you implement any of the following traits, you'll be building superior likability and making it a part of your current repertoire.

Character Traits for Superior Likability

- *Personable:* You are liked and affable; this helps you build a solid rapport with others.
- *Charismatic:* Others are captivated by and drawn to your presence.
- *Optimistic:* You bring out the best in others, regardless of the circumstances.
- *Motivator:* You easily inspire others.

Famous Examples of Superior Likability **Richard Branson**, founder and CEO of Virgin Group (which has more than 360 companies), earned a reputation as a charismatic, flamboyant, risk-taking, and adventurous entrepreneur. His larger-than-life personality makes him one of the most popular people and most emulated entrepreneurs.

Oprah Winfrey, Emmy award-winning television host, producer, and magazine publisher, is ranked as one of the richest African Americans. She gained a reputation for bringing difficult subject matter to the masses' attention and for helping to create a self-help culture with a focus on self-improvement and spirituality. Her talk-show success is attributed to the millions of viewers who find her so likable and accessible.

Questions for You to Consider *How likable are you?* Do people enjoy being with you? Do they seem drawn to and enriched by your presence? Do you put people at ease? Do they feel comfortable around you, or seem to go the extra mile for you?

What steps can you take to improve your superior likability? Some ideas might be to make yourself more available to people, or to find out about another person in whom you can take an active interest. Figure out ways to make people feel comfortable in your presence, and work toward enriching and inspiring your colleagues' lives.

Power to Persuade

> *A genuine leader is not a searcher for consensus but a molder of consensus.*
>
> —Martin Luther King Jr.
> American clergyman and civil rights leader

The power to persuade lies in your ability to convince others to follow you. When you're persuasive, you sway others to your side and win them over. They follow your direction and adopt your aspirations.

Being able to persuade others requires that you compel them to believe in you and to feel as though you have their best interests at heart. They trust the integrity you bring to a given situation, and recognize sound reasoning in your ideas. They have such strong faith in your confidence that they believe you know what you are doing. Therefore, they don't need to see you wielding authority or power. They believe in and follow you without question.

To that end, you completely believe in what you are persuading people to do. Be passionate and excited by your objectives, and share this excitement with others. This kind of enthusiasm propels people toward your point of view and prompts them to connect emotionally with your passion.

Besides passion, you also need to display confidence. Even if others doubt your ideas, they embrace them because they trust your confidence.

Persuasion involves building alliances. When your peers buy into your idea, it becomes easier for them to follow you. Seek to form bonds with people who have power and influence. If you bring them on board, others will trust the direction you're heading. You also want to collaborate with people who will share your point of view. This makes it easier for them to understand and appreciate the logic behind your persuasion.

As you implement the following traits, you'll develop a stronger power to persuade.

Character Traits for Power to Persuade

- *Persuasive:* Convince others to support and then adopt your idea or point of view.
- *Collaborative:* Encourage people to work together to create a common direction.

- *Consensus:* Gain agreement and approval from many people.
- *Alliance:* Align yourself with influential and powerful people.

Famous Examples of Power to Persuade   *Steve Jobs*, cofounder and CEO of Apple Computer and former CEO of Pixar Animation Studios, gained a reputation as a creative visionary who builds innovative technology. Throughout his career, Jobs's persuasive talents have reshaped four industries: computing (Mac, iPad); movies (Pixar); music (iPod, iTunes); and mobile phones (iPhone). His development of new products and his innovative marketing techniques create fervor in audiences who simply *have to have* these products.

Susan B. Anthony dedicated herself for 45 years to the cause of women's rights. Speaking more than 70 times in one year, Anthony earned a reputation as a prominent women's rights leader and was regarded as an organizational genius. The canvassing plan she introduced is still used by political and grassroots organizations today. Anthony's persuasion, collaborative efforts, and ability to build alliances to achieve consensus laid the groundwork for women securing the right to vote.

Questions for You to Consider   *How would you evaluate your power to persuade?* Are you able to sway your colleagues to accept your ideas? Do people believe in you and want to follow your direction? Are you passionate about your beliefs and goals? Do people readily buy into your ideas? Do you create alliances and collaborate effectively with others?

What can you do to improve on and create an increased power to persuade? Contemplate how you can convince more people to support the ideas and adopt the objectives in which you believe. Find people with whom you can collaborate on a particular project or initiative, and create an increased consensus that compels others to agree with your ideas. Be sure to align yourself with people of influence.

Summary and Action Steps

Before moving on to Chapter 10, where you'll be learning how to influence up, down, and laterally, here are the Chapter 9 summary and action steps.

Summary

- *Influence is possible for everyone.* Even without title, authority, power, or position, you can still influence others by building a solid reputation, enhancing your skill set, improving your executive presence, creating a superior likability, and leveraging the power to persuade.
- *Reputation takes time to build.* As you become more reliable and valued, your reputation improves and more people depend on you. Building a solid reputation takes time. Be diligent and patient.
- *An enhanced skill set helps you produce high-quality work and perform at a level of excellence.*
- *Executive presence convinces others to confidently follow you.* Your colleagues feed off your assured sense of self, and perceive you as powerful and effective.
- *Superior likability draws people toward you.* You lift others up with your presence, and your charismatic nature inspires others to achieve more than even they expect of themselves.
- *The power to persuade sways others to your side.* You know how to leverage collaboration and create consensus. Your persuasive skills cause others to see and agree with your point of view.

Take Action Now

- Review each of the five areas on how to become an influential person, along with the "Questions for You to Consider" sections. Block out time to answer the questions. As you focus on improving in each of the five areas, you'll immediately notice yourself becoming a more influential executive.

10

Become a Master Influencer

To lead one must influence. To be a great leader is to influence many.
—Murray Johannsen
Entrepreneur and teacher of leadership development

Influence Up, Down, and Laterally

As you have learned, influence is a major part of your success. If you don't influence others, you will not advance in an organization, and your career will stagnate. This immediate halting of career progress often shocks people; frequently, they've had such great—and quick—success in the past that they don't see this new problem coming.

Influence is a required trait for the next phase of career success. You simply cannot survive without it. Learning how to influence others is an art that takes time to hone; however, you must learn this craft and use it to your advantage. Exerting influence for the first time can often feel awkward and uncomfortable; it's almost as if you are learning to speak a foreign language that everyone else speaks and you don't. Even if you feel lost, you can begin right now to perfect your ability to grasp

> *If you don't influence others, you will not advance in an organization, and your career will stagnate.*

and work with influence. I've broken down specifically how to become a master influencer from three perspectives: up, down, and laterally.

Founder and former Visa International CEO Dee Hock explains in his book *Birth of the Chaordic Age*, "Over the years, I have frequently had long, unstructured discussions with hundreds of groups of people at every level in diverse organizations about any subject of concern to them. The conversations most often gravitate to management; either aspirations to it, dissatisfaction with it, or confusion about it. To avoid ambiguity, I ask each person to describe the single most important responsibility of any manager. The incredibly diverse responses always have one thing in common. All are downward looking. . . . That perception is mistaken."[1] Besides engaging in a "downward looking" tendency, one must also learn to manage superiors and peers.

The first area of influence is upward. Once you've become a manager, you have to focus on the people who have authority over you. You have already been aware of your boss, your boss's boss, and possibly other members of management throughout your career. Now it's time to actually focus on *influencing* these people above you. Influencing upward requires that you understand what is important to the people above you; this is a prerequisite to being promoted. The benefits of influencing upward include the fact that top management will see you as a major player in the organization. You become someone who provides value that others recognize as important, thereby augmenting your impact on the company.

The second area of influence is downward. When you move from individual contributor to some level of staff supervisor, downward influence is necessary for you to

Influencing upward requires that you understand what is important to the people above you.

manage well. This is simply about gaining as much as possible from your people, while ensuring that they learn how to take charge and know what to accomplish. You want them to step up their efforts and start doing more than what's expected of them, and to take on the kind of responsibilities they would assume at the level above where they are now. In essence, they will move toward your position. They do your work and take on your responsibilities. As they undertake your tasks, it frees you to do what is necessary at the level above your own.

The third area of influence is at the peer level. Professionals tend to focus on this area least frequently because they don't see how their peers are important components to their career success. It may seem surprising, but your peers can cause the eventual triumph or defeat of your projects and ideas. They can sabotage your proposals or be powerful supporters of them. So don't ignore the very important level of peer influence.

Martin Homlish, global chief marketing officer at enterprise application software company SAP, truly comprehends the vital importance of influencing up, down, and laterally: "When you come into a leadership role, you need to manage three ways. You need to manage down, you need to manage up, and you need to manage across—you don't forget that. If you focus all your time on managing up, you may think you're making progress with the senior leaders in the organization, but you will not have any soldiers who are going to follow you up that hill, and you won't have any colleagues who are going to stand next to you . . . the people above you will have no idea what it is you're doing, and you won't be able to get things done in the corporate environment. So,

Your peers can cause the eventual triumph or defeat of your projects and ideas.

[the balancing of all three levels of influence is] a very, very key skill to learn."[2]

Influence Up

In many ways, influencing ultimate decision makers is similar to selling products or services to external customers. They don't have to buy—you have to sell.

—Marshall Goldsmith
Author and educator specializing in leadership development

The people above you in your company are individuals you need to influence. This includes your boss and members of upper management. In short, influence anyone who has more authority than you do.

Influencing upward has benefits for: (1) the company, (2) the higher-ups, and (3) you. When you can influence upward, you help your organization as a whole achieve more. You help higher-ups become more successful in their own right, since they have another asset they can leverage on their team. They become stronger, more efficient, and more productive thanks to your added influence. As the person influencing upward, you are able to increase your effect on the company. You'll quickly notice how all your efforts affect the company, including the joy of watching others implement your ideas and witnessing their fruitful results. In addition, you gain even greater recognition and appreciation from top management, because they likely didn't expect you to be influencing to the degree that you are. You become a pleasant surprise, which helps you stand out and improves others' perception of you.

Unfortunately, not many people appreciate—or act on—the importance of influencing upward. They don't think that it's necessary, and many assume that they simply don't have time to do it. This is compounded by the fact that many of the leaders *they* observe aren't influencing upward. Many higher-ups are too consumed by the demands of daily work and performing their jobs as well as possible to focus on influencing upward. Their responsibilities, projects, assignments, and direct reports take all of their attention and time to manage—all of these are commitments that can distract them from influencing upward.

Influencing upward is often perceived as difficult because you have less positional authority than the people you are trying to influence. However, you must not buy into the belief that this should impede you in any way. You can close that gap by encouraging people to get to know you. In time, they will learn to respect you, begin to rely on you, and start to see you as one of them. As they do, the lack of authority that is merely a symptom of your position or title will become less distinguishable. As John Maxwell explains in the book *The 360 Degree Leader*, "If I had to identify the number-one misconception people have about leadership, it would be the belief that leadership comes simply from having a position or title. But nothing could be further from the truth. You don't need to possess a position at the top of your group, department, division, or organization in order to lead."[3]

A client of mine who works at Google wanted his colleagues to see him as someone who was a peer with upper management. He had built a solid reputation inside the company. People loved working with him, and he had earned a tremendous amount of respect within his business unit.

My client performed extremely well in his job. His boss felt he should take the initiative and work with his counterparts in other business units. He wanted my client to stop thinking so linearly and instead focus cross-functionally. And he wanted him to enhance his visibility with senior management.

> *You don't need to possess a position at the top of your group, department, division, or organization in order to lead.*
> —John Maxwell

My client had a high level of expertise and knowledge that gave him insight and perspective that no one else had. He received encouragement to go outside the chain of command to give his input and ideas to his boss's peers. In a short amount of time, he realized how much others valued and needed to hear his feedback and opinions. He began influencing upward toward people who now appreciated his worth. As they relied on him increasingly, they treated him as a peer—despite the fact that officially he wasn't.

In order to manage up, you need to actually understand how those above you define their own roles and success. The simplest way to do this is to ask them. Learn about the challenges they face and the aspirations they have. You have to be able to think like them, make their jobs easier, and help them succeed. Sometimes this simply requires knowing what kind of information they need and when they need it. Sometimes it means bringing them in on your own projects so that they can help solve a problem or share in a success. When done well, managing up should simultaneously make you more influential and help you produce better results, because you're both giving and receiving vital input along the way.

What You Need before Influencing Up

Setting an example is not the main means of influencing another, it is the only means.

—Albert Einstein
American (German-born) physicist and Nobel Prize winner

To influence upward, you need to gain traction in each of the following steps. Anyone who successfully influences up has mastered each step, which includes being competent, consistent, respected, trusted, and desired (see Table 10.1).

Step 1: Establish Competence This takes place when you become skilled and proficient at what you do. Others view you as a person with a high level of expertise and knowledge capital.

TABLE 10.1   Five Steps Necessary to Influence Up

Step 1	Establish Competence
Step 2	Create Consistency
Step 3	Be Respected
Step 4	Be Trusted
Step 5	Become Desired by Others

Once the higher-ups recognize your competence, they will immediately begin to develop respect for you.

Step 2: Create Consistency   When you keep proving yourself time and again, others begin to rely on your stability. Over time, this consistency creates a sense of trusted reliability from others.

Step 3: Be Respected   Others hold you in high regard. They appreciate what you do and the quality of your work. You've become someone with an established, solid reputation that others respect.

Step 4: Be Trusted   People know that they can rely on you. They are confident that you'll do what is expected of you and even more. They have complete belief in your talents and know about your abilities. No doubt exists in their minds; you are completely dependable.

Step 5: Become Desired by Others   At this point, higher-ups take an interest in you and want you on their team. They seek to have you involved in their projects and share your advice with others. They look to you to make important decisions; you become wanted and desired.

How to Influence Upward

The people responsible for your success are those above you, with the power to either promote you or block your rise up the organization chart.
—Jeffrey Pfeffer
Professor at Stanford University business school

Once you have become competent, consistent, respected, trusted, and desired, you are ready to begin influencing upward. These eight ideas will help you influence upward:

1. *Know what's important to higher-ups.* When you're aware of the significant matters and projects for senior management, you can influence what they deem important. This involves knowing their priorities, what is imperative to them, and how others are measuring their performance. This knowledge will help you determine exactly how to support them.

2. *Know the expectations of senior management.* Anticipate managers' needs by figuring out what they require and expect from you. By fleshing out clearly defined expectations, both you and upper management will know what they want and how you are going to accomplish exactly that. If you aren't aware of the expectations of senior management, you can't possibly achieve what is important to the people who have a direct impact on your success.

3. *Walk in their shoes.* Put yourself in the exact situations that the people above you face. Whether it's your boss, the CEO, or anyone else in upper management, you want to try on their jobs, do what they do, and think like they think. When you can see what they see, you will understand them better and will develop empathy for their circumstances and situations. This will greatly help you customize your management message.

4. *Tailor your message to your audience.* Each member of upper management is different, so you need to understand who each of them is on an individual basis, and what each person considers to be important. Your message needs to directly relate to their interests and priorities, and to be tailored to cover the benefits they will gain. The more relevant you make your message to the specific person with whom you're communicating, the better the chance you have of securing that person's support.

5. *Get upper management to value you.* Every interaction you have with senior managers is an opportunity to prove your worth. They need to hear about your successful projects, your key accomplishments, your value to the company, impacts you make in your department, and solutions you offer in response to challenges. Don't assume that they automatically know what is going on. Once they're aware of the contributions you make, they will realize how much they need you. Rosanne Badowski, who was Jack Welch's executive assistant at GE for 13 years, says the following about the importance of managing up: "Mastering the 'managing up' concept . . . will help in your career advancement, and it gives you an edge over the competition when you are being considered for promotions."[4]

6. *Become a strong presenter and speaker.* When you present and speak well, you are, not surprisingly, chosen to present more often, which leads to increased visibility with upper management. Being a strong presenter helps you to create immediate credibility and respect, and compels leaders to see you as more of an equal than an underling.

7. *Align your work with the strategic, big-picture plan.* Be a strategic thinker who takes a whole-company perspective. This will help you learn the organization's needs so that you can

meet them head-on. A high-level understanding of the company will help you communicate your message and prompt people in executive positions to respond to your upward influence.

8. *Find advocates for your ideas.* Being able to influence upward stimulates others to hear and implement your ideas, which directly enhances your value as the owner of that idea. So how do you break through the layers of bureaucracy to find advocates for your suggestions and concepts? Xerox's chief marketing officer, Diane McGarry, says, "Success at a big company such as Xerox requires an understanding of the many layers of office politics as well as the confidence to put your best ideas forward. You have to know which people you need to get your ideas in front of in order to get those ideas advanced."[5]

Act as though You're One Level above Your Current Position

The price of greatness is responsibility.

—Winston Churchill
British politician and statesman

The key to influencing upward is to act as if you belong at the next level. You want senior management to feel that you already possess the qualities that warrant your treatment as an equal—even if your title says that you aren't. Most companies don't promote an employee until they actually see this person completing the types of tasks and exhibiting the traits necessary to succeed at the higher level. Organizations don't want to take a risk or leap when promoting someone; rather, they want to acknowledge or reward employees for the additional responsibility they've already assumed. If higher-ups feel that you don't belong in their group—for whatever reason—this will greatly impede your ability to influence them.

One way to belong at the next level is to ask yourself: "What does my boss have ownership of that I could take over

> *The key to influencing upward is to act as if you belong at the next level.*

that would directly give me influence at his level?" You should ask yourself this question once every few weeks.

For example, if you are a senior manager who wants to become a vice president, act as if you are already a VP. Look for opportunities in your current job to complete tasks and undertake responsibilities related to the next level without being off-putting or self-inflated. I suggest in my book *Executive Presence*: "Know the type of people who hold [upper management] positions. What qualities and characteristics do they exhibit? What are their backgrounds? How do they dress, talk, behave? How do they conduct meetings? How do they respond to questions? How do they interact with those above them, [with] their peers, and with their staff?"[6]

When you belong at the next level and know how to act that way, it will create a strong foundation for you to influence up. You know how to provide input, feedback, guidance, and advice just as well as those above you.

Influence Down

Our chief want is someone who will inspire us to be what we know we could be.

—Ralph Waldo Emerson
American lecturer, essayist, and poet

As Terrance Marks, former president of Coca-Cola Enterprises, says, "A big mistake a lot of people make, and I've seen it firsthand, is they manage up well, they may manage out pretty well, but they forget about managing down."[7]

Downward influence requires that you empower the people below you and unleash their potential. By giving them the authority to make decisions, you encourage them to believe in themselves and trust their own abilities. They know that their independence is based on the confidence you have in them. Educator Booker T. Washington emphasized the importance of placing responsibility on individuals when he wrote in his autobiography, "Few things help an individual more than to place responsibility upon him and to let him know that you trust him. . . . Every individual responds to confidence."[8] Downward influence involves giving employees a vision for where you want and need them to go and then providing them with the tools and support to get there.

Luxury hotel chain Ritz-Carlton is an ideal model for creating the ultimate level of trust and belief in its people. As President Simon F. Cooper explains, "We entrust every single Ritz-Carlton staff member, without approval from their general manager, to spend up to $2,000 on a guest. And that's not per year. . . . It doesn't get used much, but it displays a deep trust in our staff's judgment. . . . There are stories about hiring a carpenter to build a shoe tree for a guest; a laundry manager who couldn't get the stain out of a dress after trying twice and then flying up from Puerto Rico to New York to return the dress personally; or when a waiter in Dubai overheard a gentleman musing with his wife, who was in a wheelchair, that it was a shame he couldn't get her down to the beach. The waiter told maintenance, and the next afternoon, there was a wooden walkway down the beach to a tent that was set up for them to have dinner in. That's not out of the ordinary, and the general manager didn't know about it until it was built."[9]

> *Downward influence involves giving employees a vision for where you want and need them to go and then providing them with the tools and support to get there.*

Downward influence will solicit the most from your employees and allow you to gain all that they are truly able to offer the company. You will be able to leverage their strengths and talents to their full capacity, while encouraging them to increase their responsibility and stretch their abilities. According to *Handbook of Leadership Theory and Practice* authors Nitin Nohria and Rakesh Khurana, "Great leaders inspire people to move beyond personal, egoistic motives—to transcend themselves, as it were—and as a result they get the best out of their people."[10]

Employees whose managers entrust them with influence want to reach their full potential. They seek added responsibility and look for ways to take risks. They want to share their views, provide advice, initiate new ideas, and solve problems in order to display their enhanced leadership ability. They want to take actions that produce results. Don Fites, former CEO of Caterpillar Inc., with over 100,000 employees, one of the largest U.S. companies, recognizes the importance of entrusting your employees with authority. He observes, "You have to distribute information, and authority, as far down in the organization as you possibly can to allow people to make the right decisions."[11] As employees continue to take on more responsibility, their confidence will increase dramatically. They become committed to and invested in the company as they continue to amplify their influence.

People who receive downward influence are usually already trusted and have earned a solid degree of respect. Leaders feel secure giving these employees important assignments and projects, and trust them to make decisions. People who are in positions of power begin to treat them as equals.

Employees today are becoming less motivated by authority or power, because they are increasingly aware that a title alone doesn't guarantee immediate respect. Most professionals nowadays have the attitude that they must earn respect regardless of position. In order for leaders to influence downward, they need to find ways to motivate, engage, empower, and stimulate their employees.

If you are a manager who must influence downward, be aware of and take an interest in your company's more junior employees. Oftentimes, the lower they are, the more they know about what *really* is going on, since these are the people who have direct contact with your products, services, customers, and clients. Listen to them, and truly hear what they have to say. They have fresh eyes and often see from a perspective much different from that of someone who is a seasoned company veteran.

How to Influence Downward

> *It would be difficult to exaggerate the degree to which we are influenced by those we influence.*
>
> —Eric Hoffer
> American social writer and philosopher

Entrusting your employees with responsibility and believing in their abilities will show that you have confidence in them. Follow these nine suggestions so you can empower your employees and gain the most from their abilities.

1. *Allow employees to be accountable for their actions.* When an employee's actions have consequences for the company as a whole, the employee develops an increased amount of support for organizational success. The employees are no longer just individuals who receive paychecks; they now feel as though they own their work. Charles Heimbold, former CEO of global biopharmaceutical company Bristol-Myers Squibb, explains: "It's not empowerment that is magic, it is accountability. Give people the responsibility and the resources to get something done. Let them understand that they will be held accountable

for it, that you are expecting those results, and that they are going to share in the success. Then watch what happens."[12]

2. *Grant more opportunities to make decisions.* Allow and encourage your employees to make important choices independently of management. Let them become responsible so that they see the results of their decision making, and ask that they rely less on going to their manager for answers. They need to feel like *they* are in charge. To do so, they must make decisions independently and self-sufficiently. This will let them see how the choices they make affect the company.

3. *Delegate important projects and tasks.* Let your employees have the projects, meetings, or tasks that others deem crucial. This will increase their visibility and help others get to know who they are.

4. *Acknowledge your employees for risk-taking behavior.* You should reward and recognize your employees for any efforts they make that surpass expectations or their current responsibilities. If they take risks or venture outside their comfort zones, recognize and encourage their actions. This will propel them to do so more frequently in the future.

5. *Target the high potentials.* Select the employees who stand out—the ones who contribute the most and constantly achieve high performance. By targeting your best people, you help them develop into future company leaders.

6. *Identify the lesser-known but equally impressive performers.* Look for individuals who perform well, but who aren't as noticeable. These are the people whom others often overlook but who are truly your organization's diamonds in the rough. With the right infusion of attention, support, and resources, you can create an outstanding top contributor who will turn into a high-potential employee.

7. *Assign stretch assignments and tasks that show confidence in them.* Employees feel respected when their managers give them stretch projects, or assignments that push them beyond their skill levels and what they thought was possible. They'll seize the opportunity to develop and continue to improve. Provide your employees with opportunities to grow and push themselves so that they increase their workload, are inspired, and produce quality results.

8. *Know what motivates your employees.* When enthused employees become active and engaged at work, they share their excitement and energy with others. In turn, this creates a more positive professional environment.

9. *Ask your employees for answers to the important problems you are trying to solve.* Treat your employees as equals by asking them to help solve your problems. They will feel empowered when you make it clear that you notice them and desire their input. Continue to seek them out and include them in important decisions on a regular basis.

Influence Laterally

When I'm getting ready to reason with a man, I spend one-third of my time thinking about myself and what I am going to say—and two-thirds thinking about him and what he is going to say.

—Abraham Lincoln
Sixteenth president of the United States

Many aspects of your work likely involve interacting with cross-functional peers to achieve successful outcomes. Even though you have no authority over them—nor have they over you—you still need to know how to enlist your peers to help endorse your projects and ideas through to completion. You can encourage your colleagues to help you meet your goals by making sure you communicate the benefits to them. You also want to leverage the respect and reputation you've earned to create buy-in.

A client of mine at Hewlett-Packard was a female senior director who wanted to become a vice president, something that both her boss and the boss's boss encouraged her to do. They felt that she was good at doing what was expected of her, produced exceptional results, and influenced both her people and her overall business unit well. While they felt she was a great leader, they worried that she lacked initiative across the company and with other business units. She received the following feedback from her boss: "You do what I tell you to do, but you don't provide influence across the company. I need to know that you have lateral influence."

My client was at a crossroads. She needed to cross the bridge and influence people *outside* of her business unit before her manager would believe she was VP material. If she couldn't successfully navigate the lateral step of influence, she would stay in her current position. She wanted that next-level VP job. She made a list of all the people she could influence laterally across the company. Then she met with her boss and his boss to receive feedback on her list. Both of them agreed to introduce her to and create visible opportunities for her to interact with the listed professionals. Within eight months her influence extended so far beyond her own professional unit that she gained the CEO's attention—and landed the VP position she wanted.

Give Help/Get Help

You stand up for your teammates. Your loyalty is to them.
You protect them through good and bad, because they'd do the same
for you.

—Yogi Berra
American League Baseball Hall of Fame player and coach

Waste Management, Inc., CEO David Steiner explains an effective strategy to create buy-in that you could also use when trying to influence your peers laterally: "The best piece of advice I ever got was from one of my directors when I first became CEO. He said, 'When you go to somebody, there's one phrase you can use that's going to help you change the culture more than anything else. . . . I need your help.' When you think, I'm the CEO and I have to come up with the ideas, you find out that your ideas fail real quickly because you're trying to impose it on someone. So, if you just use those words, 'Hey, look . . . I need your help,' and then talk with them about the issue, . . . you'll find you get some great answers and you get the buy-in, because they are the ones that are helping you put together the strategy."[13] Asking for someone's help is an invitation to be on common ground and to solve the problem together.

Besides asking your peers for help, it's equally important to go out of your way to help them. This allows you to build a robust "bank account" of favors that you can borrow against later. Look for opportunities to do something for others; make it clear that you have helped them, so that they can reciprocate sometime down the road. Don't hesitate to take advantage of career-enhancing opportunities to leverage the tokens you have amassed.

The benefits of helping your peers go beyond indebtedness. You create an environment of teamwork in which your individual needs are put aside for the common purpose of the group. You build a trusted, supportive, and collaborative relationship.

Get Your Peers' Attention

The main challenge in receiving help from your peers or providing help to them is the limited bandwidth that many of your colleagues have. A variety of forces are competing for your peers' attention. Your coworkers have responsibilities, deadlines, projects, technology (e-mail, instant messaging, voice mail), people issues, and information overload; they don't always have the time for you and your ideas. Your priorities compete with their own, and they will probably have to give up something on their end to dedicate to you and your projects.

How do you gain your peers' attention? First, you need to have a strong rapport. With a solid relationship established, your peers are more inclined to want to help you. Find ways to constantly help and support your peers. Create a balance where you are helping them at least as much as they are helping you. Then when you're competing for their attention, they will be more inclined to prioritize your needs and return the favor.

Become a Mini-CEO

The more you establish parameters and encourage people to take initiatives within these boundaries, the more you multiply your own effectiveness by the effectiveness of other people.

—Robert Hass
Pulitzer Prize–winning American poet

Leaders are finding it more and more necessary to interact and leverage their peers from different business units. Normally, they would just do the work within their own department (finance, for example) and not involve themselves in others (marketing, for example). However, many professionals are realizing how important it is to avoid becoming isolated within their departments, as this often creates an unhealthy "us versus them" mind-set. Your team will feed on this undermining perspective and resist meeting the needs and requests that come from other departments. Mike Walsh, the late CEO of equipment manufacturing company Tenneco, reinforced the importance of not just focusing on your business unit, but seeing the entire company as if you were the CEO when he said, "Every person in a key position has to see himself or herself as a mini-CEO. They have to conceptualize what has to be done in the same way the CEO has. Then it cascades."[14]

The Hay Group, a global management firm, found a direct correlation between leadership and collaboration. It conducted a study of the 20 best companies for leadership and found out exactly what differentiated these companies from the competition. The results: Their people collaborated with different parts of the organization 100 percent of the time, compared to just 66 percent from the majority of companies.[15]

Organizations nowadays recognize that mistakes and costly errors occur less frequently—and the company overall runs more efficiently—when business units are aware of and understand one another. This kind of collaboration provides much-needed support from business leaders and mutually productive intradepartmental relationships.

Understanding other departments is the key to successful peer influence. Develop connections with managers of other departments. Learn what they do, what their responsibilities are, how much influence they have, and why they are important to the company overall. Find out what is important to them, whether they feel respected as a department, and why. Discover as much as you can about other areas of your company and their people so that you can build rewarding cross-functional relationships.

In a *Harvard Business Review* blog, Chris Ernst states, "While 86 percent of the senior executives in our research said that it is extremely important that they collaborate across boundaries, only seven percent said that they did it effectively."[16] Here are a few ideas he suggests:

> *Every person in a key position has to see himself or herself as a mini-CEO.*
>
> —Mike Walsh

- Invite leaders from other units to your team meetings so they can discuss how each unit can help the other to solve pressing organizational problems.

- Set up some comfortable chairs and a whiteboard in the connector wing between two departments to encourage informal, collaborative conversations across functions.
- When divisions conflict over an issue, help them articulate the source of their differences and then explore ways to creatively reconcile them for the overall good of the organization.[17]

Former UCLA coach John Wooden, who won 10 National Collegiate Athletic Association (NCAA) national championships in 12 years, knew the importance of making sure his players understood what it was like to play a position different from their own. Gail Charles Goodrich Jr., who was on two of those 10 national championship teams, explained, "Sometimes during practice, [Coach Wooden] would have the guards switch positions with the forwards—have us do the other guy's job. He wanted everybody to understand the requirements of the player in the other positions. . . . [He] wanted the guard to appreciate the challenges a forward faced and the forward to appreciate what a guard had to deal with."[18]

Build Relationships with Other Department Leaders

The greatest ability in business is to get along with others and to influence their actions.

John Hancock
American statesman and patriot

It's necessary to establish strong connections with other departmental leaders in order to have their people and your own work effectively together. As authors Allan R. Cohen and David L. Bradford explain in *Influence without Authority*, "We have discovered that it is the process of give and take that governs influence. Making exchanges is the way to gain influence; and that process leads to cooperation rather than retaliation or refusal to engage. People cooperate because they see something of value that they will gain in return."[19]

Begin now to identify and build relationships with peers of yours who you believe will be future company leaders. These are the individuals whom others respect, and who are at the cusp of advancement. As you climb the corporate ladder together, you'll be able to support and leverage each other toward the successful outcomes you both desire.

A client of mine who was a manager at Deloitte identified a peer who was a star employee going places, and also happened to be a manager. They were in different offices; one was in Dallas and the other in New York. Each person respected the other greatly, and knew how talented they were. The relationship evolved into an extremely supportive one. Eventually, they were e-mailing or speaking to each other daily. They both moved up to become senior managers, and eventually became partners in the firm at the same time. They supported each other's success as their careers progressed. Eight years later, they are now partners in the same office.

It is essential to find peers like this for yourself, whom you respect and with whom you can establish a strong connection. If you advance in the company, they will be right there with you to share in the success. Forming close relationships with your peers will multiply rewards as all of you move ahead together. You will do whatever it takes to move projects forward. You'll keep to time lines and produce top-notch results. Often, success involves the collaboration of people in multiple departments, which is precisely why having strong relationships with their managers is vital. When other business units understand the value of your department to the overall company, their respect for you and motivation to help grow exponentially.

One of my clients at Wells Fargo Bank told me she needed to build relationships with other company-unit leaders. During her coaching session, I asked her to identify a business challenge she was facing and to invite another department's leader to help her brainstorm a solution. Her colleague provided a unique point of view to my client's problem. The relationship deepened and their mutual respect grew. The two peers became more aware of each other's talents and continued to support each other throughout their banking careers.

You must build relationships and collaborate with your peers across departments. By working with them, you will gain support for your ideas and initiatives. Additionally, your organization will enjoy increased success when you are able to work across departments. The benefits of peer influence prompt the following to occur:

- You accomplish projects and action items quickly.
- You create innovative ideas.
- You solve problems and challenges.
- Productivity grows due to shared knowledge and resources.
- You enjoy invaluable support and understanding from a range of colleagues and departments.

How to Influence Laterally

> *Accept the fact that we have to treat almost anybody as a volunteer.*
> —Peter Drucker
> American writer, deemed the father of modern management

Enlisting your peers' support is a vital component to influence. Your peers are the ones who can make or break the success of your ideas, suggestions, and projects. Review and implement these 13 points to begin laterally influencing right now.

1. *Join forces with your cross-functional departments.* Find projects and tasks that will help unite you with other departments.

This will help to leverage their knowledge capital and resources.

2. *Hold your peers accountable to high standards.* When everyone is responsible for a company's success, employees across the organization will achieve a higher standard of work. Your peers will respect and appreciate when you challenge them to accomplish more, enhance their skills, and experience greater success. It isn't supportive to allow your colleagues to take it easy. If you see them slacking off, find out why and help them become motivated and reengaged.

3. *Gain buy-in for your ideas and initiatives.* Present your ideas to your peers with the intention to generate buy-in. Gaining support across business units provides you with strength to compel others to accept your ideas. This occurs when you're able to understand and incorporate others' perspectives, and present your initiatives from this point of view. When your peers consent to your ideas, you'll reap outstanding results.

4. *Build an extremely wide lateral sphere of influence.* You want as many allies as possible—more than you think you need. It can be devastating when an important ally is fired or decides to leave the company, especially if this ally is your boss and he or she has been your biggest advocate. Therefore, make as many connections in as many departments as you can. Gather enough allies so that if one or two leaves you will still have a large network of support.

5. *Support your peers.* Be there for your colleagues by providing guidance and counsel. Reach out to them to see if they need support, and lend your time and resources as required. This will come back to you tenfold, as your efforts create an intention of mutual support and goodwill.

6. *Watch out for threats to your peers and protect them.* Make an effort to protect your peers from others' inaccurate or harmful perceptions. You want to "have their backs."

Garner the courage to speak up and defend your peers if or when someone says or does anything to undermine their influence.

7. *Provide feedback.* Honest commentary about areas of concern and improvement will benefit your peers. Being at the same level as your peers makes it easier for them to truly hear your opinions and suggestions, and for the mutual respect you share to grow.

8. *Work through any cross-functional issues that arise.* Your objective is to resolve the issue as quickly as possible, and to maintain an open and honest relationship. Be direct and earnest in your attempt to understand your colleague's perspective. Ensure that you take responsibility for any actions on your part that might have caused the conflict to arise.

9. *Understand your peers.* The better you understand your peers, the stronger your alliances with them will be. Some questions for you to consider about your peers include: With whom do they have alliances? What is important to them? What objectives are they trying to achieve at this time? How does your group benefit them?

10. *Provide constant recognition and acknowledgment.* Your peers need to know that others appreciate them; chances are that their work goes unrecognized more often than it should. It helps them feel valued when someone they respect provides much-needed acknowledgment. This is especially important when influencing your peers or leading a project in which they are participating.

11. *Respect your peers' responsibilities and priorities.* Everyone has their own responsibilities, which demand attention and time, as well as having a bottom line for which they are held accountable. Your peers' current commitments and tasks may not lead them to want what you want. Be aware and respectful of your peers' situations and circumstances.

12. *Eliminate competitiveness.* Look for ways to be collaborative and inclusive with your peers. Be open and revealing with your agenda so that everything is transparent. Forming a cooperative relationship full of support and assistance creates a mutually beneficial and effective work environment.

13. *Align yourself to many groups—not just one.* It's easy to become attached to one specific area of your company. You may be drawn to a few people in one group and then latch on to them. Interacting with a variety of departments, however, will help you when the influence of one of them is diminished or eradicated. Rely on multiple groups, and create a coalition to champion your ideas and projects.

Summary and Action Steps

Before moving on to the concluding chapter, where you'll learn how a person can combine perception, visibility, and influence to achieve greatness, here are the Chapter 10 summary and action steps.

Summary

- The three kinds of influence on which you need to focus are *up*, *down*, and *lateral*. As you leverage these three areas, you'll become a master influencer.
- Influence upward to the people who have authority over you. The people above you are able to experience your leadership and appreciate its impact. As you influence up, they recognize and value your worth more. You will also begin to see the impact you have on the organization.

- Influence downward to the people you supervise. You are able to maximize your employees' potential and talents. As they learn to better utilize these traits and abilities, you will have more free time to work on the key areas of your job.
- Influence at the peer level. Once you realize how much information and how many projects involve your peers, you appreciate the importance of establishing strong cross-functional relationships to secure your success.

Take Action Now

- Reread the "Influence Up" section and evaluate your effectiveness in this area. Write down some areas in which you do well, and some upon which you must improve.
- Go over the five steps in the section "What You Need before Influencing Up." Review each trait and create one action step you can accomplish that would help you embody that specific trait more fully.
- Review the section "How to Influence Upward" and select two ideas from the list. Block out time right now to turn each idea into an action plan that you will implement over the next 30 days.
- Look for opportunities in your current job to complete tasks fulfilled at the next level. Ask yourself once every few weeks, "What does my boss have ownership of that I could take over that would directly provide me influence at his level?" You might even put an alarm reminder in your PDA or smart phone.
- Review the "Influence Down" section, and evaluate your effectiveness. Schedule 30 minutes in the next 10 days to record what you do well and what you can improve in this area.

- Review the ideas in the "How to Influence Downward" section, and select one task to carry out in the next 48 hours. Stop everything you are doing—even reading this book. Take this action step right now and complete it within two days.
- Share the "Influence Laterally" section with a colleague or peer. Discuss together what you both learned after reading this section. At the end of the discussion, write a summary of what you do well and what you both need to work on when influencing laterally. Create one action step to which both of you are willing to commit.
- Review the list of ideas in the "How to Influence Laterally" section. Share this list with your immediate boss during your next one-on-one meeting or take it to your next performance review. Together, select three ideas from the list that your boss will commit to helping you implement during the next month.

Bonus Online Material

How well do you exert your influence at work? Take the free assessment at www.GarfinkleExecutiveCoaching.com/assessments-influence.html to find out. Through this evaluation, you'll learn the top 10 areas you must emphasize to be influential.

The PVI Model in Action

A True Story

Don't wait. The time will never be just right.

—Napoleon Hill
American author specializing on achieving success

Howard Lincoln woke up in his hotel room in Las Vegas. He was heading to the world's largest consumer technology trade show, the Consumer Electronics Show (CES), at which he was going to be the main speaker. As chairman of Nintendo, Lincoln was to make a major announcement that had the place buzzing with anticipation: *Nintendo was going to partner with Sony to create a new home video game console.* Many Sony executives couldn't wait for the announcement and had been promoting the product the night before while bragging about the partnership between Nintendo and Sony.

The announcement, however, didn't go as Sony employees had hoped or claimed. Instead of partnering with Sony, Nintendo announced that it was partnering with Philips N.V., the Dutch electronics giant. The news sent shockwaves throughout the conference. Nintendo had betrayed one Japanese company (Sony) for a European company (Philips), a breach that violated the cultural norms of the Japanese business world. Not only that, but Philips was actually Nintendo's rival. Nintendo's reputation took a big hit as a result.

The Impact

This event directly affected a 38-year-old Sony engineer named Ken Kutaragi. As the Sony project leader who led the effort to design a home video game product, Kutaragi's dreams nearly died when Nintendo turned down the partnership with his company. However, he didn't let this stop him. He took the initiative and formed a Sony team to build its own home video game console in direct competition with Nintendo. The product he created turned out to be the Sony PlayStation, which went on to sell more than 100 million units.[1]

Today, Ken Kutaragi is known as the father of the PlayStation. In response to his brainchild, Sony created an entire gaming division, of which Kutaragi was put in charge and which soon became Sony's number-one business unit. At one point, it brought in 60 percent of Sony's operating profits.

Kutaragi's story exemplifies how perception, visibility, and influence are catalysts to advancement. He went from taking his first postcollege job at Sony all the way up to becoming chairman and CEO of Sony Computer Entertainment.

The Secret to Kutaragi's Success

Kutaragi achieved the right perception early in his career by proving himself in high-profile areas such as LCD displays and digital cameras. He compelled others to see him as a highly intelligent problem solver and a skilled engineer. Kutaragi encouraged this perception by turning Sony CEO Norio Ohga into an advocate who would speak on his behalf. He was able to encourage the CEO to acknowledge his contributions publicly, which helped improve the perception of him within the company.

Kutaragi was also outspoken, which was rare in the Japanese culture at that time. His tendency to share his opinion candidly enhanced his profile across the organization. He stood out, got noticed, and received high-level attention and rewards from his superiors.

The key turning point came when Kutaragi saw his daughter playing with a Nintendo game console. He was inspired by what he saw and realized the incredible potential of video games. When he spoke with managers at Sony about video games, however, they quickly shot down his ideas. They felt that video games were a fad, and rejected efforts to develop that technology. Phil Harrison, who worked at Sony and later became president of Sony Computer Entertainment Worldwide Studios, said, "Sony's old guard was scared that video games were going to destroy this wonderful, venerable, 50-year-old brand. They saw Nintendo and Sega as toys, so why on earth would they join the toy business? That changed a bit after we delivered 90 percent of the company's profit for a few years."

Refusing to be deterred by the lack of internal support at Sony, Kutaragi created a sideline project with Nintendo to work on a revolutionary sound chip for its video game console. Besides creating one for Nintendo, he also designed one for Sony. It's somewhat shocking that he would work with Nintendo—the very organization that had betrayed him at the Las Vegas show by surprisingly partnering with Philips. Ken believed so much in his project, however, that he took the risk. He did this while working at Sony and without the knowledge of Sony executives because he knew they would reject his efforts. This risk he took very well could have cost him his job. Instead, it guaranteed his success and sealed his legacy.

When Sony executives found out about the sideline partnership, they were furious. Fortunately for Kutaragi, however, he had established a level of visibility all the way to the top of the Sony organization. CEO Norio Ohga therefore approved and supported the project. At the meeting in which Kutaragi revealed the Nintendo relationship, the following took place: "When Ohga asked what sort of chip it would require, Kutaragi replied that it would need one million gate arrays, a number that made Ohga laugh. Sony's production at the time could only achieve 100,000. But Kutaragi slyly countered with: 'Are you going to sit back and accept what Nintendo did to us?' The reminder enraged Ohga all over again. 'There's no hope of making further progress with a Nintendo-compatible 16-bit machine,' he said. 'Let's chart our own course.'"[2]

Father of the PlayStation

Kutaragi now had the influence he needed. He had risked his career and led a charge for something that no one else realized was so important to Sony's future success. Kutaragi didn't just take the lead on the project; he bet his entire career on it, and it worked.

Kutaragi's dedication to his idea in the face of opposition led to one of the greatest impacts one person can have on an established and major corporation like Sony. For that very reason, he is a model for building and exerting influence.

Kutaragi is an example of what is possible when you combine perception, visibility, and influence. He used all three of these concepts to their full capacity—and accomplished the highest level of success and impact possible as a result.

Your Time Is Now!

While aimlessly waiting for their so-called ship to come in and change their life for the better, far too many people miss the boat that could actually carry them to a brighter future. They are often so afraid of testing new waters that they spend an entire lifetime waiting on the shore. . . . Begin your journey now!

—Josh Hinds
Author and speaker

Everything you've learned throughout the pages of this book will serve as a catalyst for reaching the next rung on the ladder of career success. You have everything you need—all the strategies, insights, tools, and tips to move ahead. The PVI model is your guiding light throughout your entire career, so you can maximize your potential and realize your professional greatness.

What makes one person more successful than another? This book started with that question, and you now know the answer. You know how to be more successful. You have clarity and conviction on exactly how to leverage and apply perception, visibility, and influence better than anyone else. The PVI model is the competitive advantage that will allow you to stand out from the talented stars surrounding you.

You know how to fast-track to the next level. Be a valued employee. Be a leader who is in demand. Advance and achieve your deserved promotions. Take on greater responsibility and visibly important projects. Become recognized as extremely capable, credible, and highly respected by upper management. Be a person of influence.

The far-reaching success you desire at work is now a real and attainable possibility. You believe in yourself more than ever. Your confidence is off the charts. Whatever you want is within your grasp. Now, go after it. Leverage all that you have learned from this book. The time to seize the opportunities waiting for you is now.

> *The PVI model is your guiding light throughout your entire career, so you can maximize your potential and realize your professional greatness.*

May you soar to levels in your career beyond imagination as you climb swiftly and powerfully upward, reaching career heights you have never before deemed possible.

Notes

Introduction

1. *Partners of the Heart*, PBS film, February 2003, www.pbs.org/wgbh/amex/partners/filmmore/fd.html.
2. *Partners of the Heart*, PBS film, February 2003, www.pbs.org/wgbh/amex/partners/filmmore/pt.html.
3. Seth Godin, *The Big Moo: Stop Trying to Be Perfect and Start Being Remarkable* (New York: Penguin Group USA, 2005).
4. Nitin Nohria and Rakesh Khurana, *Handbook of Leadership Theory and Practice* (Boston: Harvard Business Press, 2010), 657.
5. James M. Citrin, *The Dynamic Path: Access the Secrets of Champions to Achieve Greatness through Mental Toughness, Inspired Leadership, and Personal Transformation* (Emmaus, PA: Rodale Books, 2007), 65.
6. John C. Maxwell, *The 21 Indispensable Qualities of a Leader: Becoming the Person Others Will Want to Follow* (Nashville, TN: Thomas Nelson, 2007), 22.
7. Michael Phelps and Alan Abrahamson, *No Limits: The Will to Succeed* (New York: Free Press, 2009), 108.

Chapter 1 Power of Perception

1. "Alfred Nobel," *Wikipedia*, accessed September 25, 2010, en.wikipedia.org/wiki/Alfred_Nobel.
2. Ronald Chan, *Behind the Berkshire Hathaway Curtain: Lessons from Warren Buffett's Top Business Leaders* (Hoboken, NJ: John Wiley & Sons, 2010), 132.
3. Laura Sabattini, "Unwritten Rules: What You Don't Know Can Hurt Your Career," Catalyst, June 2008.

4. Mike Myatt, "Perception Matters," August 16, 2010, www.n2growth .com/blog/.

5. Jeffrey Pfeffer, "Shape Perceptions of Your Work, Early and Often," *Harvard Business Review* blog—*The Conversation*, October 21, 2010.

6. Nielsen Company, "Internet & Social Media Consumer Insights," June 14, 2010, www.nielsen.com/us/en/insights/pressroom/2010/nielsen_ and_mckinsey.html.

Chapter 3   The Four-Step Perception Management Process

1. Carlin Flora, "The First Impression," *Psychology Today*, May 14, 2004.

2. Umesh Ramakrishnan, *There's No Elevator to the Top* (New York: Portfolio, 2008), 208.

3. Marshall Goldsmith, *Leadership Effectiveness: Provide Feedback and Follow Up* (Provo, UT: Executive Excellence, 2003).

4. Ramakrishnan, *No Elevator*, 93.

5. Bill George, *True North: Discover Your Authentic Leadership* (San Francisco: Jossey-Bass, 2007), 74.

6. Mark Murphy, "Pixar's Secret for Delivering Tough Feedback," *Leadership IQ*, January 23, 2011, www.leadershipiq.com/thought-leadership/ blog/article-pixar%E2%80%99s-secret-for-delivering-tough-feedback.

7. Sharon Daniels, "For a Better Career Outlook, Look Inward," *Harvard Business Review* blog—*The Conversation*, September 2, 2010.

8. Barbara Pagano, Elizabeth Pagano, and Stephen Lundin, *The Transparency Edge: How Credibility Can Make or Break You in Business* (New York: McGraw-Hill, 2003), 39.

9. *Harvard Business Review on the Tests of a Leader* (Boston: Harvard Business Press, 2007), 50.

10. Ramakrishnan, *No Elevator*, 22.

11. Frank Dell'Apa, "Bryant Scores Off an Assist," *Boston Globe*, June 18, 2010.

12. Ibid.

13. Adrian Wojnarowski, "Scout's Eye Helped Bryant Focus on Title Drive," *Yahoo! Sports*, June 17, 2009.

14. *Harvard Business Review on Leadership* (Boston: Harvard Business School Press, 1998), 125.

Chapter 4   Up Your Visibility

1. Georgia Flight, "How They Did It: Seven Intrapreneur Success Stories," *BNET.com*, April 10, 2008.

2. Seth Godin, *Purple Cow: Transform Your Business by Being Remarkable* (New York: Portfolio, 2003), 3.

3. Dorie Clark, "How to Become a Thought Leader in Six Steps," *Harvard Business Review* blog—*The Conversation*, November 9, 2010.

4. Jeffrey Pfeffer, *Power: Why Some People Have It and Others Don't* (New York: HarperBusiness, 2010).

5. George W. Dudley and Shannon L. Goodson, *The Importance of Managing Visibility* (Dallas, TX: Behavioral Sciences Research Press, 2002), 3, salescallreluctance.com/Visibility%20Management.pdf.

6. Pamela Weinsaft, "Voice of Experience: Monica Mandelli, Managing Director, Investment Management Division, Goldman Sachs," *Glass Hammer*, September 21, 2009.

7. Pamela Weinsaft, "Voice of Experience: Melissa Goldman, Managing Director, Goldman Sachs and Head of Credit Risk, Collateral Management and Cross Divisional Projects, Technology," *Glass Hammer*, May 13, 2010.

8. Hayagreeva Rao, Robert Sutton, and Allen P. Webb, "Innovation Lessons from Pixar: An Interview with Oscar-Winning Director Brad Bird, *McKinsey Quarterly*, April 2008.

9. Paula Keaveney, *Marketing for the Voluntary Sector: A Practical Guide for Charities and Non-Government Organizations* (London: Kogan Page, 2001).

10. Adapted from Pfeffer, *Power*. www.jeffreypfeffer.com/pdf/Power DosandDonts-Pfeffer.pdf.

11. Barbara Kantrowitz and Vanessa Juarez, "When Women Lead," *Newsweek*, October 24, 2005.

12. Sylvia Ann Hewlett, "When Female Networks Aren't Enough," *Harvard Business Review* blog, May 12, 2010.

13. "One Woman's Advice to Another: It's Always Time to Speak Your Mind," *Knowledge@Wharton*, March 30, 2011, http://knowledge.wharton.upenn.edu/article.cfm?articleid=2746.

14. Joanna Barsh and Susie Cranston, *How Remarkable Women Lead: The Breakthrough Model for Work and Life* (New York: Crown Business, 2009), 231.

15. Russell Freedman, *Give Me Liberty! The Story of the Declaration of Independence* (New York: Holiday House, 2000), 62.

16. Carmen Nobel, "Introverts: The Best Leaders for Proactive Employees," *HBS Working Knowledge*, October 4, 2010.

17. Adam M. Grant, Francesca Gino, and David A. Hofmann, "Reversing the Extraverted Leadership Advantage: The Role of Employee Proactivity," *Academy of Management Journal*, forthcoming, http://journals .aomonline.org/InPress/main.asp?action=preview&art_id=858&p_id= 1&p_short=AMJ.

18. Ibid.

Chapter 5   Promote Your Success

1. Mallory Stark, "Creating a Positive Professional Image," *HBS Working Knowledge*, June 20, 2005.

2. Anne Fels, "Do Women Lack Ambition?" *Harvard Business Review*, April 2004.

3. Kate McClaskey, "Take More (Calculated) Risks: Five Ways to Build Your Risk Instinct and Get Ahead," *Glass Hammer*, July 30, 2010.

4. N. Tal-Or, "Bragging in the Right Context: Impressions Formed of Self-Promoters Who Create a Context for Their Boasts," *Social Influence* 5, no. 1 (2010), 23–39, doi:10.1080/15534510903160480.

5. Joel Garfinkle, "Executive Presence: Practical Strategies to Stand Out, Be Noticed and Get Ahead," 2009, www.garfinkleexecutivecoaching. com/executivepresence.html.

6. Jeffrey Pfeffer, "Shape Perceptions of Your Work, Early and Often," *Harvard Business Review* blog—*The Conversation*, October 21, 2010.

7. Keith H. Hammonds, "Copy This," *Fast Company*, March 1, 2005.

8. Robert I. Sutton, "Why Good Bosses Tune In to Their People," *McKinsey Quarterly*, August 2010.

9. Fels, "Do Women Lack Ambition?"

Chapter 6   Speak Up, Speak First, and Speak Often

1. Andrew S. Grove, *Only the Paranoid Survive: How to Exploit the Crises Points That Challenge Every Company* (New York: Crown Business, 1999), 115.

2. Jeffrey Kluger, "Competence: Is Your Boss Faking It?" *Time*, February 11, 2009.

3. Joanna Barsh and Susie Cranston, *How Remarkable Women Lead: The Breakthrough Model for Work and Life* (New York: Crown Business, 2009), 199.

4. Nilofer Merchant, "Three Times You Have to Speak Up," *Harvard Business Review* blog—*The Conversation*, February 3, 2011.

5. Heidi Evans, "Ursula Burns to Head Xerox, Will Be First Black Woman to Be CEO of Fortune 500 Company," *New York Daily News*, May 22, 2009.

6. Jodi Glickman, "How to Interject in a Meeting," *Harvard Business Review* blog, November 3, 2010.

7. Carolyn Kepcher, "Talk Your Way to the Top: Good Communication Skills Are Key to Advancing Your Career," *New York Daily News*, August 23, 2010.

8. "One Woman's Advice to Another: It's Always Time to Speak Your Mind," *Knowledge@Wharton*, March 30, 2011, http://knowledge .wharton.upenn.edu/article.cfm?articleid=2746.

Chapter 7   Raise Your Profile

1. Carolyn Kepcher, "Talk Your Way to the Top: Good Communication Skills Are Key to Advancing Your Career," *New York Daily News*, August 23, 2010.

2. Bob Nelson, *1001 Ways to Take Initiative at Work* (New York: Workman Publishing, 1999), 2.

3. *Harvard Business Review on Leadership* (Boston: Harvard Business School Press, 1998), 185.

4. Jim Collins, *How the Mighty Fall: And Why Some Companies Never Give In* (New York: HarperCollins, 2009), 160.

5. Hay Group, Best Companies for Leadership study, 2011, www .haygroup.com/BestCompaniesForLeadership/.

6. Thomas J. Neff and James M. Citrin, *Lessons from the Top: The 50 Most Successful Business Leaders in America—and What You Can Learn from Them* (New York: Crown Business, 2001), 274.

7. Abrahm Lustgarten, "14 Innovators," *Fortune*, November 15, 2004.

8. Howard Schultz, *Pour Your Heart into It: How Starbucks Built a Company One Cup at a Time* (New York: Hyperion, 1999), 210.

9. Paul F. Nunes, Tim Breene, and David Smith, "A Team You Can Count On," *Outlook*, February 2011.

10. Anne Morriss, Robin J. Ely, and Frances X. Frei, "Managing Yourself: Stop Holding Yourself Back," *Harvard Business Review*, January–February 2011.

11. John Zenger and Joseph Folkman, *The Extraordinary Leader: Turning Good Managers into Great Leaders* (New York: McGraw-Hill, 2009), 163–164.

12. Adam Bryant, "Never Duck the Tough Questions," *New York Times*, July 17, 2010.

13. Umesh Ramakrishnan, *There's No Elevator to the Top* (New York: Portfolio, 2008), 20.

Chapter 8   Lead through Influence

1. Jeremy Schaap, "We Will Catch Excellence," *Parade*, February 3, 2008.

2. Noel M. Tichy, *The Leadership Engine* (New York: Harper Paperbacks, 2002), 191.

3. Nitin Nohria and Rakesh Khurana, *Handbook of Leadership Theory and Practice* (Boston: Harvard Business Press, 2010), 193.

4. Roy Johnson and John Eaton, *Influencing People* (New York: Dorling Kindersley, 2002).

5. Linda A. Hill, "Becoming the Boss," in *Harvard Business Review on Developing High-Potential Leaders*, 149 (Boston: Harvard Business Press, 2009).

6. Charles Handy, in *The Leader of the Future*, ed. Frances Hesselbein, Marshall Goldsmith, and Richard Beckhard, 6 (San Francisco: Jossey-Bass, 1996).

7. Andre Brink, "Nelson Mandela," *Time*, April 13, 1998.

8. Stephen Ambrose and Douglas Brinkley, *Witness to America: An Illustrated Documentary History of the United States from the Revolution to Today* (New York: HarperCollins, 1999).

Chapter 10   Become a Master Influencer

1. Dee Hock, *Birth of the Chaordic Age* (San Francisco: Berrett-Koehler, 2000), 68.

2. Umesh Ramakrishnan, *There's No Elevator to the Top* (New York: Portfolio, 2008), 202.

3. John C. Maxwell, *The 360 Degree Leader* (Nashville, TN: Thomas Nelson, 2006), 4.

4. Elizabeth Garone, "What It Means to 'Manage Up,'" *WSJ.com*, October 30, 2008.

5. "You Are Your Brand: Defining a Personal Leadership Style," *Knowledge@Wharton*, January 14, 2005.

6. Joel Garfinkle, *Executive Presence: Practical Strategies to Stand Out, Be Noticed and Get Ahead*, 2009, www.garfinkleexecutivecoaching.com/executivepresence.html.

7. Ramakrishnan, *No Elevator*, 48.

8. Booker T. Washington, *Up from Slavery: An Autobiography* (Sioux Falls, SD: NuVision Publications, 2007).

9. Robert Reiss, "How Ritz-Carlton Stays at the Top," *Forbes*, October 30, 2009.

10. Nitin Nohria and Rakesh Khurana, *Handbook of Leadership Theory and Practice* (Boston: Harvard Business Press, 2010), 192.

11. Thomas J. Neff and James M. Citrin, *Lessons from the Top: The 50 Most Successful Business Leaders in America—and What You Can Learn from Them* (New York: Crown Business, 2001), 126.

12. Ibid., 173.

13. Robert Reiss, "Saving the Planet While Generating Profit," *Forbes.com*, May 3, 2010.

14. Noel M. Tichy, *The Leadership Engine* (New York: Harper Paperbacks, 2002), 22–23.

15. Hay Group, *Report of the 2010 Best Companies for Leadership Study*, 2011, www.haygroup.com/BestCompaniesForLeadership/downloads/2010_Best_Companies_for_Leadership_Report.pdf.

16. Chris Ernst, "Finding Innovation in the Flattened Organization," *Harvard Business Review* blog—The Conversation, January 28, 2011.

17. Ibid.

18. John Wooden, *Wooden on Leadership: How to Create a Winning Organization* (New York: McGraw-Hill, 2005), 132.

19. Allan R. Cohen and David L. Bradford, *Influence without Authority* (New York: John Wiley & Sons, 1991), 23.

The PVI Model in Action

1. "The Making of PlayStation," *Edge*, April 24, 2009.

2. Ibid.

Resources

Speaking Services

Book Joel to energize and educate your keynotes, meetings, conventions, and seminars with his compelling and inspirational speaking style.

www.JoelInspirationalSpeaker.com

Coaching Services

Joel provides five coaching services that address people in different stages of their careers. These services include:

Executive coaching

www.GarfinkleExecutiveCoaching.com

Dream-job career coaching

www.DreamJobCoaching.com

Job coaching

www.dreamjobcoaching.com/coaching/job

Salary negotiation coaching

www.dreamjobcoaching.com/coaching/salary-negotiation-strategies

Executive outplacement services

www.Outplacement-Firm.com

Articles

Free articles that provide practical, "how-to" information and insights to help you become an effective leader and boost your career success.

80+ FREE articles on executive leadership:
www.garfinkleexecutivecoaching.com/articles.html

200+ FREE articles on career transitions and dream jobs:
www.dreamjobcoaching.com/resources/articles

Newsletter, Blog, Twitter

By signing up for the newsletter, blog, and twitter, you'll gain articles, tips, and quotes from industry leaders.

Fulfillment@Work E-mail Newsletter
www.dreamjobcoaching.com/resources/newsletter

Blog
www.CareerAdvancementBlog.com

Twitter
www.Twitter.com/#!/WorkCoach4You

About the Author

Joel Garfinkle is recognized as one of the top 50 coaches in North America. His valuable insight has been sought after by companies, including Google, Amazon, Hewlett-Packard, Gap, Starbucks, Deloitte, Cisco Systems, Oracle, Bank of America, Citibank, Microsoft, and many more.

Joel is the author of seven books and more than 300 articles on leadership, executive presence, getting ahead at work, career transitions, and work fulfillment. He is regularly featured in the national media, including ABC News, National Public Radio, the *New York Times*, *Forbes*, the *Wall Street Journal*, *Business-Week*, *Kiplinger's Personal Finance*, *Newsweek*, and *Fast Company*.

For more than two decades, Joel has had firsthand experience advising thousands of executives, senior managers, directors, and employees at the world's leading companies. He draws from this experience to provide coaching programs that serve individuals and organizations throughout the world.

Joel is also a sought-after speaker who conducts workshops, trainings, and keynote addresses that empower corporate audiences. He has delivered more than a thousand customized presentations that provide fresh insight into common issues that employers and employees face.

Before starting his company, Joel worked as a consultant for Ernst & Young in Hong Kong and at Andersen Consulting (now Accenture) in San Francisco.

Joel publishes a popular bimonthly newsletter *Fulfillment@ Work*, which is delivered to more than 10,000 subscribers in 25 countries around the world. He also is the author of six powerful and transformative books:

- *Executive Presence: Sixteen Characteristics to Help You Advance Up the Corporate Ladder Quickly and Effectively through Increased Exposure, Visibility, and Self-Promotion*
- *Time Management Mastery: Stress-Free Productivity in the 7 Key Areas of Life (Time, Projects, People, Schedules, Information, Work/Life Balance, and Abundance)*
- *Get Paid What You're Worth: How to Negotiate a Raise or Higher Starting Salary*
- *Land Your Dream Job: The Last Career Search Book You'll Ever Need*
- *Love Your Work: Make the Job You Have the One You've Always Wanted*
- *Find a Job in 14 Days: A Practical Guide and Process for Finding the Job You Need, Fast!*

Joel has worked and lived in London and Hong Kong. He currently lives in the San Francisco Bay Area with his wife, Jueli, and their two children, Ariella Joy and Haydn Kol.

Index